Summital Pluricast Pathwrighting in Wanderwebs

Asher

Summital Pluricast Pathwrighting in Wanderwebs

First Edition September 2025

Written by Asher

TABLE OF CONTENTS

CHAPTER NO.		TITLE	PAGE NO.

CHAPTER NO.	TITLE	PAGE NO.

CHAPTER NO.	TITLE	PAGE NO.

CHAPTER NO.	TITLE	PAGE NO.

CHAPTER NO.	TITLE	PAGE NO.

LIST OF TABLES

TABLE NO.	TITLE	PAGE NO.

LIST OF FIGURES

FIGURE NO.	TITLE	PAGE NO.

FIGURE NO.	TITLE	PAGE NO.

FIGURE NO.	TITLE	PAGE NO.

LIST OF SYMBOLS AND ABBREVIATIONS

AAM	-	Associativity based Ad Hoc Multicast
ACK	-	Acknowledgement
ABT	-	Acknowledgement based Busy Tone
AMRP	-	Ad Hoc Multicast Routing Protocol
AODV	-	Ad Hoc On-Demand Distance Vector
AGDA	-	Adaptive delay & Cross-layer based routing Algorithm
ALMP	-	Application Layer Multicast Protocol
APLM	-	Application Layer Multicasting Protocol
ABR	-	Associativity Based Routing
BEMP	-	Bandwidth Efficient Multicast Protocol
BMMP	-	Batch Mode Multicast Protocol
BMWM	-	Broadcast Medium Window MAC
CTS	-	Clear-to-Send
CH	-	Cluster Head
CM	-	Cluster Member
C-MRP	-	Cross-Layer based optimal Multicast Routing Protocol
DSDV	-	Destination Sequenced Distance Vector
DDMP	-	Differential Description based Multicast Protocol
DCF	-	Distributed Coordination Function protocol
DMR	-	Dynamic Multicast Routing
DSR	-	Dynamic Source Routing
EEHD	-	Energy Efficient Hybrid Distributed
E-COPS	-	Energy Efficient Scheduling Algorithm
FAR	-	Flow Augmentation Routing
FIP	-	Fuzzy Inference Process
FBROP	-	Fuzzy logic Based stable multipath Routing Protocol

GAFP	-	Geographic Adaptive Fidelity Protocol
GRP	-	Geographic Routing Protocol
GPS	-	Global Positioning System
IP	-	Internet Protocol
LAN	-	Local Area Network
LAMP	-	Location Aware Multicast Protocol
LIC	-	Lowest Identification Clustering
MAC	-	Media Access Control
MER	-	Minimum Energy Routing
MANET	-	Mobile Ad Hoc Network
MOBICA	-	Mobility based metric Clustering Algorithm
MAODV	-	Multicast Ad Hoc On-Demand Distance Vector
MMP	-	Multicast sensitive MAC Protocol
MSM	-	Multicast Sensitive MAC protocol
MBQ	-	Multicasting Broadcast Query
NS	-	Network Simulator
ODMRP	-	On-Demand Multicast Routing Protocol
OOMA	-	On-demand Overlay Multicast Algorithm
OMMR	-	Online Max- Min Routing
OTP	-	Optimal data Transmission Path
OLSRP	-	Optimized Link State Routing Protocol
PDR	-	Packet Delivery Ratio
PLR	-	Packet Loss Ratio
P2P	-	Peer to Peer
PLRP	-	Power aware Localized Routing Protocol
PASDM	-	Progressively Adapted Sub-tree for Dynamic Mesh
PENP	-	Prototype Embedded Network Protocol
QoS	-	Quality of Service
RBT	-	Receiver side Busy Tone

RMMP	-	Reliable Multicast MAC Protocol
RSM	-	Reliable Sender-initiated MAC
RTS	-	Request-to-Send
SMP	-	Stable Multipath Routing
TORP	-	Temporally Ordered Routing Protocol
WMP	-	Weight based Multicast protocol
ZRMP	-	Zone Routing based Multicast Protocol

CHAPTER 1

INTRODUCTION

This chapter briefly discusses an outline of various classifications of routing protocols exercised in MANETs, common classes of its functions, advantages and disadvantages of each routing protocol, and applications of MANETs, important metrics considered for effective route establishment, motivation, scope and objectives of this thesis work. This chapter also presents the challenging issues in the current research which is clearly discussed.

1.1 PREAMBLE

Today, many organizations profoundly want to make use of the available useful information among their employees who are separated geographically in a proficient and dynamic manner. Typically, a computer network has offered this service and now plays a vital role in almost every modern business. Required with features, an organization has two options for setting up a computer network. One can employ a wired network in which all the nodes or computers and other networking devices are completely connected by using networking cables. Second, the organization may setup a network which uses radio waves to connect all devices including computers. A wireless network permits an organization to become more flexible and mobile. Thus, organizations in the modern world are now exploiting the features offered by wired networks and wireless networks to converse and share data rapidly. A wireless network uses radio waves instead of wires to make communication between nodes which is a suitable option for business or home networking. In addition, any individual or organization might employ this choice to develop their existing wide area wired or entirely wireless. One of the noted points about wireless network is allowing devices to communicate without any networking cable with the intention of offering mobility with restricted coverage area. There are two main classifications of wireless networking techniques: infrastructure less and infrastructure based.

An ad-hoc wireless network as shown in Figure 1.1 composed of many computers each integrated with a special wireless network interface card. Thus, each computer is capable of making direct communication with all other wireless facilitated computers. All wireless equipped devices can share resources like files, printers, etc., however may not be permitted to access wired resources. But, this incompatibility can be avoided by enabling one of the devices as a bridge connected to the wired network using special software.

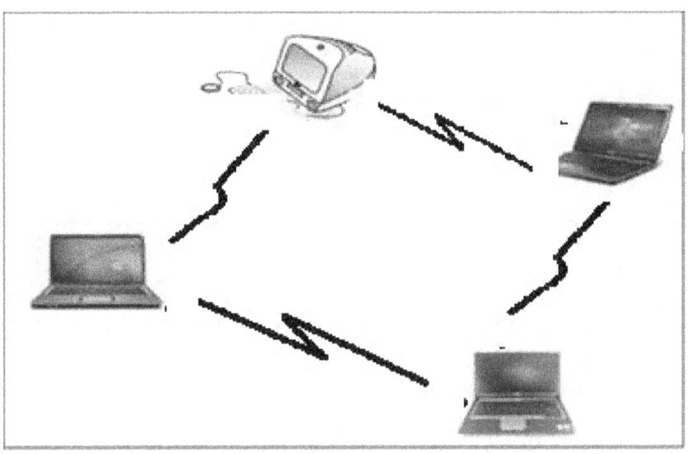

Figure 1.1 An Ad Hoc wireless network

1.2 MANET

A Mobile Ad Hoc network (MANET) is a wireless network, which encompasses of both mobile and fixed nodes, which are connected wirelessly and do not rely on any central administration or permanent infrastructure. In this kind of network, the access point provides connectivity between wireless computers. In addition, it can also be a bridge to connect a wired LAN to a wireless LAN, permitting wireless computer to communicate and access LAN resources like file servers, existing Internet services, etc. as shown in Figure 1.2.

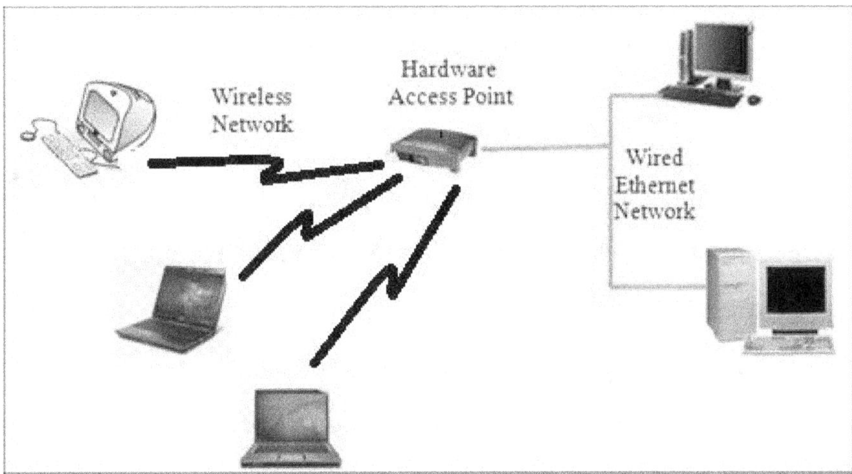

Figure 1.2 Infrastructure based ad-doc wireless network

MANETs include numerous prominent characteristics: dynamic network structure, flexibility, discovery of optimal route, robustness, rapid deployment, high mobility support, restricted capacity, unidirectional/ asymmetric links, and scarcest battery power. MANETs are successfully suitable for many fields such as civil appliances (e.g., traffic applications, video conferencing, disaster management), military operations (e.g., planes, instant message communication, structure of teams, tanks), and adjoining with cellular network (Toh2002;Perkis 2000;Deering1989).

Multicasting is one of the important roles in MANETs to bear aforementioned application areas that offer group communication service. Through multicasting mechanism, a datagram can be delivered to a cluster of mobile hosts discovered by a unique destination address. However, ensuring reliable datagram service,i.e., delivery of datagram to all mobile hosts of a cluster is important (Chiang 1998). Multicasting in a MANET uses broadcasting property of wireless technology to offer many benefits by improving the effectiveness of the communication channel and reducing the communication cost. This is achieved by transmitting many redundant data in single transmission, minimizing channel capacity preservation, delivery delay, and energy consumption.

The mechanism of multicasting in MANET is more challenging than wired network. Multicasting also faces many challenges such as varying characteristics of the wireless channel, movable members of multicast group and restricted energy and transmission power (Gerla*et al.* 1999). The multicast route discovery protocols designed and implemented in wired infrastructure are not suited to Ad Hoc environment due to handling the problems like dynamic route change, frequent link breakage and contradictory characteristics of the transmission medium.

Researchers (Chiang *et al.* 1997, Shen&Jaikaeo2005) have proposed solutions for handling multicasting in MANET's using wired mechanism. However, such approaches failed to get improved throughput and stability due to rapid node mobility. This leads to the requirement of exploring other strategies for MANETs. Many multicast route discovery protocols have been presented in the past in which each protocol is designed with different principles and functions.

1.3 DESIGN CHALLENGES AND ISSUES OF ROUTING PROTOCOLS IN MANETs

The complexity of designing a multicast route discovery protocol for MANETs is a challenging problem. Because, these multicasting protocols must be designed to handle many issues like limited energy and power resources, number of nodes presented in the current network (i.e., capacity), dynamic topology changes, high bit-error rate, and hidden terminal issues. Some of the important requirements that need to be considered when designing a multicast route discovery protocol are listed below.

1.3.1 Mobility, Robustness, and Topological Structure

Dahal andRay (2016) proposed that the nodes in a MANET can freely join and leave the network at any time at diverse speed. The sustained and dynamic movement of the mobile nodes decided the structure of the network. A multicast route discovery protocols for MANETs should be highly robust in handling topological changes due to mobility of mobile nodes with restricted capacity; thus can circumvent dropping of data packets during multicast data transmission and reduce packer delivery rate. At the same time, it is vital to reduce control overhead when establishing and upholding the network.

1.3.2 Effectiveness and Capability

Compared to traditional networks, the network capacity, multipath fading, and inference are three properties that characterizes the performance of MANETs. Design of proficient multicast routing protocols (Yang &Zan 2013) should be capable of handling a huge number of control packets like acknowledgements proportional to the number of data packets transmitted by the source node. In addition, the mechanism to increase and improve the capacity of the current network is also important.

1.3.3 Energy Conservation

Managing power and energy consumption of mobile nodes in a MANET is one of the important considerations. Researchers (Gouda*et al.* 2012) describe that nodes in a MANET do not have stable power supply system and have to rely on restricted power supply. The life time of the current network is decided by the movement of nodes and frequently changing their position and exhausted batteries. Therefore, the power and energy saving mechanisms seek to minimize the total power and energy consumption of the entire multicast group,i.e., reduce the total number of mobile nodes selected for establishing a multicast connection and also maximizing its life time.

1.3.4 Quality of Service Model for MANETs

With the growth of real-time applications for MANETs, ensuring Quality of Service (QoS) is the most important design issue. The multicast route discovery protocols designed for MANETs should be able to make use of many important network possessions to attain QoS like capacity, packet loss , delay and jitter.

Because of the peculiarity in characteristics of a MANET (Yang &Zan2013), it will be very difficult to accomplish all of these QoS needs at the same time. Even if all requirements can be achieved, the protocols will not look simple; rather need to suffer from many issues such as high power and energy conservation, high operating cost, need of maintaining many routing table information, etc. Therefore, reservation based QoS mechanisms will not be appropriate for MANETs than adaptive nature.

1.3.5 Reliability and Security

Researchers (Mohamed *et al.* 2015)propose that reliability is very essential in multicasting, specifically for applications like military operations, emergency operations, etc. And it is very difficult to offer reliable data service to the members of a network whose structure varies instantly. A multicasting protocol that offers reliability should be able to detect origin of errors, type of error message, and retransmission mechanism being implemented. As MANETs use open wireless communication medium with any central controller, security is another very important factor during multicasting. Therefore, protection of individual component of a MANET from inference, man-in-middle attack, denial of service attack, spoofing, eavesdropping, etc. can be achieved by implementing security features either at the application layer or network layer.

1.3.6 Routing Scalability

All nodes in a MANET have excellent sensing power, transmitting power and receiving power and can route packets to all its intermediate nodes in the network (Murthy andManoj2004). Among various existing network architectures, a MANET has magnetized a lot of consideration in different real-time applications, where wired network failed to setup. Typically, MANETs have no centralized device to control functions such as data transmission, forwarding, congestion control, etc.

These constraints create routing as a challenging problem in MANETs. In this environment, each node includes all function to forward data or control packets to the next immediate hop and permitting them to reach the destination node through multiple hops. In addition, each node may operate as router, source node, destination node and can move unreservedly in any direction and thus making rapid and irregular topology. All nodes in

MANET are operated with limited battery power through a great assortment in their ability. Thus, conserving an individual node's power and energy is a crucial design problem and also becoming a challenging issue.

The nodes that recline within each other's communication range can do communication directly and also responsible for dynamically learning each other. However, to permit communication between nodes which don't fall within each other's radio coverage can use intermediate nodes. The important problems like energy consumption and transmission band become the root cause for node disconnection and rerouting. This problem can be resolved through multi-hop communication technique where source node can send data packets to its communicating node using intermediate nodes. However, a node requires more energy to communicate its destination node which is located too far.

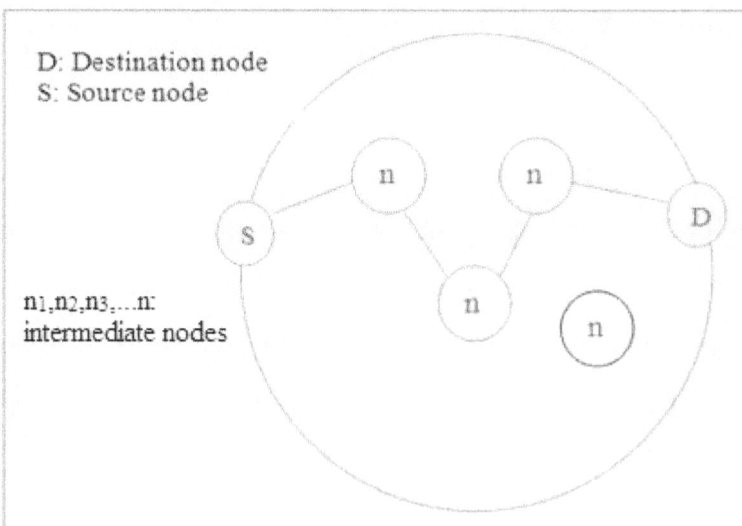

Figure 1.3(a) Route formation at time *T* between S and D

The communication range is directly propositional to the energy requirement of a node (Haenggi 2003). However, a MANET encounters larger hop count to make data transmission complete.

Recently, implementing wireless based applications becomes a timely requirement and also popular. There are many routing discovery protocols proposed for the MANETs by researchers in the past. However, performance of a MANET becomes a crucial part of its design. This is because of its dynamic topological changes. Even, movement or disconnection of a single mobile node in a pre-established path increases route complexity problem, thereby affecting the performance of the whole network.

Though, passive routing protocol like AODV handles node disconectivity problem by implementing route discovery mechanism, restarting the same path many times causes problems like redundant paths and nodes as shown in Figure 1.3.

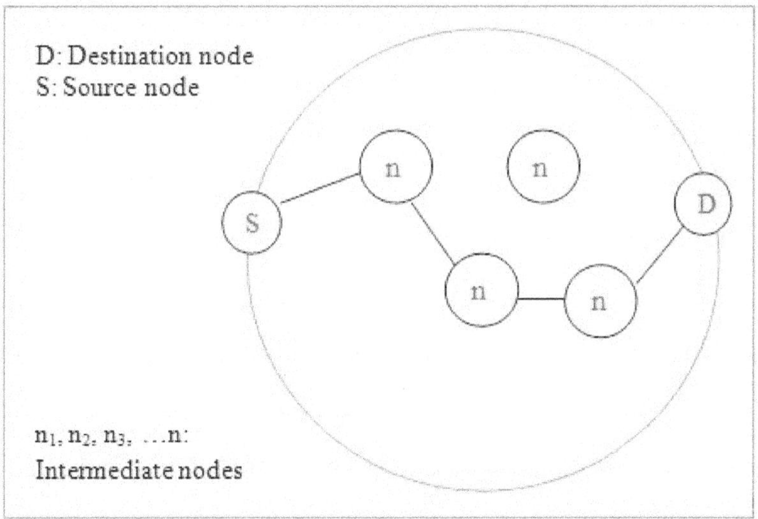

Figure 1.3(b) Route formation at time (T+Δt) between S and D

In MANETs, node density is one of the network conditions that affect the performance of a multicasting protocol. A multicast route discovery protocol should be designed to support scalability to certain level in a MANET by considering important characteristics (random mobility, power limitation, etc.).

1.4 ORGANIZATION OF MULTICAST ROUTE DISCOVERY PROTOCOLS

A multicast route discovery protocol can be designed to offer an acceptable level of reliable data service in a MANET with a dynamic and huge quantity of mobile nodes. The design of such issue should also consider the important characteristics of the Ad Hoc network (e.g., capacity, power and energy limitations, mobility of nodes, etc.).

Protocol designers and researchers focused on designing many different protocols that can be implemented at suitable layers of the protocol stack in which each layer performs specific functions and services. For example, the network layer is typically responsible for routing or transmitting data between two communicating devices, the application layer can store data temporarily until acknowledgement packet had been received, and the MAC layer ensures reliable data service. Existing MANETs multicast route discovery protocols belong to different categorizes (Wang *et al.* 2008, Junhai*et al.* 2008, Chen and Wu 2003, PapavassiliouandAn 2002, Perkins 2000) but mostly fall into three important classifications based on its layer functions, namely, application layer multicasting, network layer multicasting and MAC layer multicasting as shown in Figure 1.4.

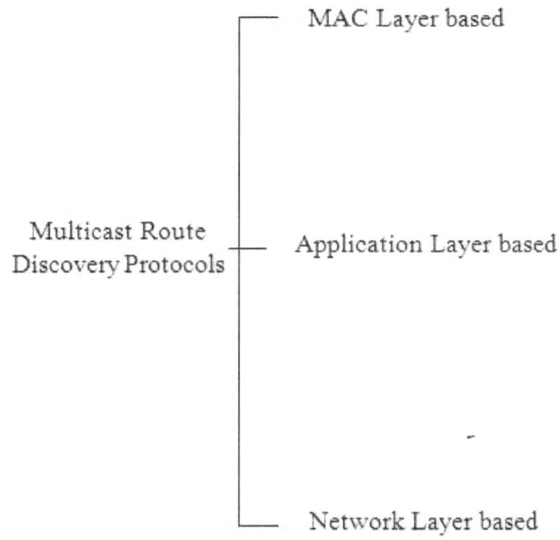

Figure 1.4 Categories of multicasting protocols

1.4.1 Application Layer Multicasting

The Application Layer Multicasting Protocol (APLM) has contributed a little in MANETs (SinhaandBharghavan1999, JetchevaandJohnson2001,Lee *et al.* 2002,Biswas and Nandy, 2004, Kim andKim2005). The most important features offered by the APLM are listed below.

- As the APLM does not need the support of the network layer, making deployment simple.
- An intermediate node does not require retaining per-group state information locally.
- Establishment of virtual topology handles problems associated with routing process.
- APLM offers many lower layer services like congestion control, flow control, reliability and security depending on the context of application areas.

The two important problems related to APLM are robustness and routing efficiency. The former issue deals the process of distributing multicast tree that depends on the total number of end nodes present in the network. The second issue handles the method of delivering several replicas of multicast packets by using each available physical link. As, all multicasting packets are broadcast by one member of a group to another member in the same group or another member of different group as unicast data packet, low resource consumption and high rate of collusion may result specifically when network density is high. In addition, the source node may not be aware of increase in intermediate hop count from the source mobile node. The broadcasting nature of APLM mechanism can help to improve routing efficiency to certain extent (Perkins andBhagwat1994; Chiang1998).

1.4.2 Network Layer Multicasting

Multicasting protocols can also be designed and effectively applied at network layer (i.e., IP protocol) of the protocol stack (Gerla*et al.* 1999, Royer andPerkins2000,Lee andKim2000, Wang *et al.* 2001, Das *et al.* 2002,Sajama andHas 2003, CaiandYang 2003, Zhang andJacob2004, StanzeandZitterbart2005,Santi2005,NguyenandXiong2005, Cai*et al.* 2006). The network layer offers the best effort data service and also responsible for transmitting received data packets between source nodesand the exact destination node. Therefore, this layer requires cooperation and support of all nodes of a MANET and intermediate forwarders to maintain information about their group state.

1.4.3 MAC Layer based Multicasting

Typically, all multicast packets routed from source mobile node to its communicating nodes use multiple intermediate hops. As wireless communication links are delay and error prone, it is difficult for an intermediate hop to receive a multicast data packet as received from its neighbouring node. Therefore, error handling and revitalization methods need to be installed on an upper layer through an acknowledgement control packet or notifying failure of such multicast data packets to the destination node. This mechanism requires all intermediate hops including the (source, destination) pair to follow store-and-forward mechanism until multicast data packets successfully reaches the destination node without improving the delay time. The increase in the total number of intermediate hop count, leads to the increase in the each node's buffer size (Perkins andBhagwat1994). The multicasting protocol being implemented at MAC layer always aims to improve MANET's efficiency through incorporating mechanism like retransmission and positive acknowledgement, i.e., ensuring reliable data service.

1.5 CLASSIFICATIONS OF MULTICAST ROUTE DISCOVERY PROTOCOLS

The multicast route discovery protocols designed for MANETs typically fall under three main categories: proactive, reactive, and hybrid as shown in Figure 1.5.

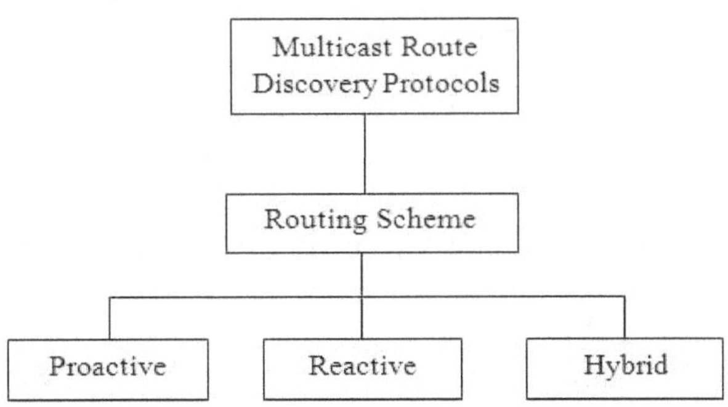

Figure 1.5 Classification of routing schemes

1.5.1 Proactive Routing Protocols

Table-driven based multicast route discovery protocols rely on retaining reliable and current multicast route discovery information connecting all members of the group in the underlying network. This was achieved by maintaining one or more local routing table. If any intermediate node receives any recent routing information, immediately updates the information in its routing table and broadcasts the same to all its immediate neighbouring nodes. This event can be done periodically. Thus the routing table of each node in a MANET always contains most recent and consistent view of the network. When a sender node wants to transmit a multicast data packet to its communicating node, it uses the known routing information and forwards the packet immediately. These kinds of protocols are usually called *proactive* routing protocols.

Proactive routing protocols normally make use of distance vector or link-state algorithm to construct routing tables that contain details about all destinations, number of intermediate hops to reach the destination, and next hop. Existing protocols such as Fisheye state routing protocol (Perkins 1997), destination-sequenced distance vector (Pei *et al.* 2000), and dynamic sequence routing belong to proactive type. The above mentioned algorithms have different number of local routing tables and they use different mechanisms for exchanging routing table information.

As proactive protocols always try to maintain information about current topological changes, they require more power, high capacity, and significant control overhead. Specifically, in wireless network the topology of the network changes dynamically. However, proactive routing protocols cause minimal routing latency, because a route established most recently is constantly accessible for the source node to reach the members of a multicast group.

1.5.2 Reactive Routing Protocols

In this kind of routing protocol, each member in a network ascertains or preserves a route information based on-demand. This type of protocols, routes are established only when a node wants to transmit data packets (reactively). To achieve this, on-demand protocols follow two important procedures: route discovery and route maintenance. During route discovery process, the sender node that has data for transmission send route-request control packet to all its neighbouring nodes which then forward the received packets to all neighbouring nodes, and the process is repeated until the control packet reaches the destination node. After receiving the route-request packet, the destination node responds by transmitting route-reply control packet using the same route as received by the route-request control packet. Once the data transmitting path has been established, route maintenance process begins in which each intermediate node keep routing information in a route-cache.

The advantage of using reactive protocols is that it requires minimal routing information and incurs minimal control overhead, and uses low capacity and power. But the limitations are that these protocols fabricate enormous amount of control packets during route discovery process, and higher latency due to topology changes which happens recurrently in MANETs. Few examples, of on-demand routing protocols are Ad-hoc On Demand Routing (AODV) (Rahman*et al.* 2012), Dynamic Source Routing (DSR) (Rahman*et al.* 2012), and Associativity Based Routing (ABR) (AcevesandMadruga1999) protocols.

1.6 HYBRID ROUTING PROTOCOLS

Hybrid multicast route discovery protocols combine the features of both proactive- and reactive-based multicasting protocols but also avoid and improve the important issues of each. An accurately designed proactive multicast route discovery protocol method and an accurately designed reactive multicast route discovery protocol can be deployed at any hierarchical level.

In addition, a hybrid routing protocol follow Inter-Zone mechanism,i.e., maintaining the structure of the network around a radius through table-drive mechanism and Intra-zone is using the on-demand routing approach. This approach makes a node that sits outside of the network to wait for longer time to become a member of a multicast group. Based on the idea of route construction process in a MANET, multicast route discovery protocols can be classified into different type as discussed below.

1.7 TREE-BASED ROUTING PROTOCOLS

In tree-based routing method, only a single communication path is established between the source node and destination node. There exist two different types of tree-based protocols: source tree based and shred tree based. In the former type, the source node is responsible for creating a multicast spanning tree for all nodes of a group. Typically, the communication path between the source nodes and any member of the multicast group is not the shortest. In case of shared-tree based model, a single multicast tree is generated for one multicast group that consists of all source mobile nodes. The root of this tree is called as core node. A source node can use this tree to initiate the multicasting process. On the other hand, shared tree model is not efficient during multicasting process. In this model, the route between the source mobile node and the destination mobile node is very rarely the shortest.

Also, this model causes more overhead, maintains additional routing information, and prone to single point of failure. Also, the traffic is collected and kept in a central buffer for further analysis on the shared tree approach instead of evenly distributing throughout the ad-hoc network. Besides, multicasting protocols which use shared tree approach need appropriate protocol functions to handle network separation and merging. But, shared tree based multicasting protocols do not need such defined operations, since the network separation that includes the source node maintains the shared multicast tree. Although the shared tree based protocols suffer from scalability issue, it offers high throughput rate, because the traffic load is equally distributed in the network.

1.8 MESH-BASED ROUTING PROTOCOLS

In this type, first a multicasting mesh that connects a source node to all its receiver nodes in the network is manipulated. There exist multiple routes from the source node to each destination node. Such redundant routes improve packet throughput rate and become resilient to robustness (i.e., link failure). However, mesh-based approaches introduce problems like power wastefulness, capacity surplus, and transmission overhead, because of redundant information/packets. Compared to mesh-based approach, the tree-based scheme saves both power and energy, but liable to link failure. On the other hand, the mesh based multicasting method is well suited to MANETs than tree based approach.

Hybrid based approach combines both the tree-based method and the mesh based method to attain both efficiency and robustness. Both approaches caused overhead during the construction and maintenance of delivery of the mesh or multicast tree, specifically in an environment where network topology changes frequently. To address this problem, the stateless based approach has been proposed in the past (Chiang *et al.* 1998, Sinha and Bharghavan, 1999,Kim andKim2005) by retaining all routing information in the packet header field instead of keeping them locally in each forwarders. Stateless based approach is well suited for a small sized multicast group. Generally, packet may become loss in a MANET due to frequent communication link failure, and lack of high mobility of nodes. To maintain a multicast group more efficiently, it is necessary to follow either the hard-state mechanism or the soft-state mechanism.

In case of soft-state based mechanism, the existing multicast group member's routes are refreshed regularly by flooding the control packets. But the hard-state based approach is very efficient and effective by reconfiguring and deploying each broken link using two different schemes. In first scheme, namely reactive, the established routes are importantly reconfigured by transmitting control packet through the broken link. On the other hand, in second type namely, proactive where the link failure can be determined by sending GPS signal and reconfigured before link failure occurs. As the proactive based scheme produces higher packet delivery ratio than reactive based scheme, it is more consistent.

1.9 IMPORTANT METRICS OF A MANET PROTOCOL

Many issues associated with power, energy and routing are incorporated in each node of a MANET. All such issues are the design and development of a protocol in MANETs. Indeed, discussing a routing path between a source mobile node and its communicating node faces a few difficult issues due to the requirement of optimize energy and power consumption, comply with the restricted capacity of the nodes and ensuring high quality of services. These issues are rooted by many factors like technology applied, throughput, stability, power and energy conservation, quality of service, etc.

1.9.1 Restricted Capabilities

The restricted capabilities of the nodes in a MANET, local buffer, energy, and power prevent the design development of more complex mechanisms, and completely running on powerful batteries increase its size. Similarly, one of the key recommended issues to take into consideration is to optimally use the energy and power consumed during the route discovery process and the maintenance of the same route in reverse direction. In addition, a few vital methods employed to discover optimal and stable route are: the broadcasting methods employed, data exchange procedure employed, transmission of power control of the nodes, and energy saving approaches, which result in extending the life time of a MANET.

1.9.2 Size of the Network

The number of nodes of a MANET is often important, and its topology frequently changes with the failure or the addition of some nodes sensors. This change in topology requires maintenance and a regular update of patterns of management of routes. Also, the reorganization of the network and the updating of routing tables, or sometimes the change in the approach of routing used according to the new data, involves the participation of a vast number of sensor nodes, which is hard to manage by routing protocols.

1.9.3 Dynamicity of Topology

In a MANET, the location of each node is not static, i.e., nodes can freely move anywhere at any time with variable speed at erratic time. Thus, the structure of the topology may vary randomly. Each node in a MANET needs to energetically establish a route to its communication node or group.

Maintaining routing information among nodes locally requires regular updates of the status of each neighbouring links. Nevertheless, any factor such as the environmental conditions can affect the quality of wireless medium and lead to vanishing of the existing links between any two nodes which may alter the entire routing process.

1.9.4 Energy and Power Consumption

Energy and power play a vital role in deciding the life time of the underlying topology in MANETs. In order to transmit data packet, a source node might use low power if the destination node appears closer,i.e., the distance between the source-node and the destination-node decides the power being utilized. Energy is another important metric to be used during route establishment and maintenance process. Discovering an optimal route between any two nodes is very important. Thus, a node in a MANET can have four different states: broadcast, receive, sleep and idle where each state can represent different level of energy conservation.

1.9.5 Multi-hop based Data Transmission

In MANET, nodes can exchange data packets with each other through wireless links. In addition, nodes must get assistance from its neighbouring nodes by forwarding each other control or data packets, probably involving several intermediate hops. This permits the nodes that cannot have direct communication path to exchange data through intermediate node without wasting its transmission power. While using intermediate nodes for data transmission, the sender node can save transmission power, thus minimizing interference effects. When multiple nodes are concerned during an end-to-end path establishment, it is more important to minimize control overhead during each single packet transmission.

1.10 APPLICATIONS OF A MANET

Due to the increase in cellular and wireless devices, the Ad Hoc wireless networks gain more importance that include military and commercial sectors etc. The Ad Hoc Networks permit users to access and exchange data even where there is no possibility of installing infrastructure. Table 1.1 lists some well known applications possible for a MANET and additional information on how it is used in a specific application. Nowadays, MANETs are not just exercised for critical real-time applications, but are also being utilized for necessary and domestic applications.

Table 1.1 Applications of a MANET

S. No.	Area of Application	Purpose for Deployment
1	Military Strategic Operations	For speedy and possibly quick establishment of secret communications and the way of deploying troop in intimidating and/or strange environments.
2	Disaster Assistance Operations	To enable communication in environments specifically where the active infrastructure is ruined or inoperable.
3	Search and Salvage Operations	To setup communication infrastructure in areas Specifically with little or no wireless infrastructure support.
4	Law Enforcement	To ensure fast and secure communication during implementing law enforcement operations.
5	Commercial Use	To enable communications in remote conferences, exhibitions, and instant gatherings. In case of some business circumstances, the requirement of mutual collaboration outside of office might be more useful than inside an office block.
6	Sensor Networks	Supervision home and office appliances through MANETs in the case like nearby, distantly, etc. And tracking of things such as living thing and weather sensing allied activities
7	Educational sector	Preparation of communications services for computer made conference rooms or smart class rooms.
8	Backup Services	Liberty functions, tragedy revival, replacement of static infrastructure diagnosis or data recoding in hospitals

1.11 MOTIVATIONS OF RESEARCH

There are few issues with routing process in mobile ad-hoc network. Many popular real-time applications require optimal multicasting and stable route and reliable data transmission with high throughput.

As the nodes in a multicast group can freely move in and around the coverage area of a MANET, the structure of its topology can dynamically change over time as in the case of wireless networks. This becomes the root cause for many problems like link failure, and redundant links. However, introducing relay nodes between the source node and the destination node can overcome this issue but can't be an ideal solution.

In addition, discovering a healthy mobile node in terms of keeping maximum power level and energy level is very important and challenging issue.

1.12 OBJECTIVES OF RESEARCH

The more critical and challenging issue in MANETs are establishing energy and power efficient multicasting route with fewer intermediate hop count because the operating time of mobile nodes is the crucial limiting feature. In recent years MANET applications are widely admired and are applied in many areas. Design and development of energy and power efficient multicast routing protocols are still immature.

Hence, this research work has two key objectives. The first objective of this research work is to develop an optimal route discovery algorithm for MANETs to offer better throughput and improved network life time than existing algorithms in each type. The second objective of this thesis work is to design a cross-layer based multicast route discovery protocol using fuzzy logic which optimizes the power and energy consumption during data transmission between the source node to the destination node or members of a multicasting group. Thus, the proposed research work is carried out with the following objectives.

- To design and develop a new multicast route discovery algorithm for MANETs to offer better results than the existing algorithms in the task optimal route establishment category.
- To formulate the cross-layer based multicast route discovery protocol or approach for MANETs with the aim of minimizing the use of power and energy consumption during routing, maximizing throughput, and stability, thus improving the life time of entire network.

1.13 PROBLEM STATEMENT

Based on the aforementioned objectives, the cross-layer based multicasting route discovery problem is formulated. It consists of two important components namely, an energy efficient route detecting algorithm and cross-layered multicasting protocol that rely on fuzzy system for making decisions and defuzzification process. The energy efficient route detection algorithm is an input to the cross-layer based multicasting protocol that determines a stable route from a source node to the destination node or members of a group with high throughput and high packet delivery ratio.

1.14 SCOPE OF RESEARCH

Any fine research experiment has span for future research just about its relevant in application domains. The reach of the methods proposed in this research work are not restricted to the application domains like military operations and monitoring; commercial purpose, etc. Multicast data communication using distributed systems are planned for future research.

1.15 OUTLINE OF THE RESEARCH CONTRIBUTION

In this research work a new multicasting route optimization algorithm has been developed for MANETs.

Further, the cross-layer based multicasting route discovery problem for MANETs has been formulated and the solution is provided by utilizing fuzzy-logic based rule system for MANETs.

(i) Power and energy efficient route discovery algorithm namely, Optimal data Transmission Path (OTP) Algorithm has been developed. The OTP algorithm is compared against the traditional and existing algorithms such as MOBICA, LIC, and E-COPS. The comparison based on energy, maintenance, packet delivery ratio, throughput and delay shows that the proposed OTP algorithm outperforms the existing solutions in terms of exercised metrics.

(ii) A fuzzy decision based multicasting protocol namely, Cross-layer based optimal Multicast Routing Protocol (C-MRP) has been proposed for MANETs to overcome the issue of ad-hoc multicast on-demand table-driven routing protocol. The proposed C-MRP approach is compared with AODV, ODMRP, and PDTMRP protocols. The comparison results point out that C-MRP provide better results than other existing solutions.

1.16 ORGANIZATION OF CHAPTERS IN THETHESIS

The current chapter investigates the research problem by reciting the different network types used for data communication in MANETs, categorizes of protocols applied, important metrics, and applications. The motivation, scope of the thesis, objectives and problem statement of the thesis work are also described. A concise summary of the various chapters of the thesis is listed below.

Chapter 2 describes the survey on various multicasting protocols. This chapter is arranged into several sections such as multicasting protocols for MANETs, classification of existing multicasting protocols used in MANETs, some related works about energy efficient routing protocols exercised in MANETs.

Chapter 3 presents the proposed OTP algorithm. The performance of the OTP algorithm is derived and explained. Various performance metrics are used for evaluating the proposed OTP algorithm. Finally, the performance of the OTP algorithm is compared against the existing algorithms and the results attained by different tests are presented.

Chapter 4 exemplifies the cross-layer based multicast route discovery algorithm developed for MANETs. Subsequently, the experimental results with an objective to maximize the life time of a MANET, offering stable route establishment with optimal power and energy efficient, maximizing throughput, and packet delivery ratio are presented. Finally, the simulated experimental results are compared with existing and some traditional protocols. Also this chapter presents a comparative analysis showing the efficiency of the proposed protocol.

Chapter 5 proposes AODVOPL protocol for link prediction to estimate the availability of active link to the neighbouring nodes. Based on this information, when link failure is expected between two nodes, proactively an alternate path is built up even before the link breaks.

Chapter 6 proposes a cross layer design for Power Optimization and Link Availability Prediction (POLAP) protocol for mobile Ad Hoc networks that provides solution for power optimization and link availability.

Chapter 7 concludes the thesis work by accenting the results that are assisted to achieve the objectives. The limitation of this research work has been recognized to carry out the promising future research work.

CHAPTER 2

LITERATURE SURVEY

This chapter briefly discusses a survey of the various traditional multicasting routing protocols, energy and power efficient routing protocols for MANETs. The limitations of the existing multicast routing protocols or algorithms and the importance for developing a new energy and power optimized multicast routing protocol are also pointed out. The most challenging issues and the necessities for the development of cross-layer based optimal route detection are also emphasized in the succeeding sections.

2.1 PREAMBLE

In mobility based wireless ad-hoc networks, if a destination mobile node might is out of radio coverage range of a source mobile node, a routing scheme is always required to discover a path to forward the data packets correctly between the source mobile node and the destination mobile node. In a cellular network, all mobile nodes can reach the base station through broadcasting (i.e., without routing). But, in the case of wireless ad-hoc network, each mobile node must be itself able to forward all received data packets to all neighbouring nodes. This issue becomes the root cause for creating more problems including dynamic and unpredictable topology changes (Feeney 1999, Schiller2000). There are a few serious research works have been carried out for MANETs with different aspects like routing, power control and energy management, and security implementations, and so forth.

The basic goal of a MANET is the ability to work in multi-hops, thus intermediate mobile nodes taking the responsibility of forwarding packets to the intended destination node. Thus, trust worthiness and cooperation between intermediate mobile nodes have become an important issue. In specific, establishing energy aware routing may become the vital design criteria of a MANET, this is because mobile nodes are battery powered with limited capacity. Power shutdown of a mobile node in a MANET has not only has effect on the mobile node but failed to forward the packets on behalf of other nodes and hence reduce the overall life time of the entire network. Therefore, many researchers have focused on developing energy efficient routing protocols.

2.2 TRADITIONAL MANET ROUTING PROTOCOLS

The multicast routing protocols in MANETs are employed to discover a path from source node to intended destination node. Numerous protocols have been proposed for MANETs in the past. The existing multicast routing protocols can be categorized in many modes, but mainly these are classified depending on either the method of routing strategy applied or its network structure (Royer andToh1999). According to the routing policy applied, all routing protocols falls under three important types: proactive multicast routing protocols (Boukerche*et al.* 2011,Rahman*et al.* 2012), reactive multicast routing protocols and hybrid multicast routing protocols (Lal*et al.* 2011). The following sections briefly present the working principle and comparison of some existing traditional routing protocols designed for MANETs.

2.2.1 Destination Sequenced Distance Vector Protocol

The DSDV multicast routing protocol belongs to proactive multicast routing protocol that relies on modified Bellman-Ford algorithm.

DSDV adds a new element namely, sequence number, to the routing table at each mobile node. The local routing table, which is retained at each mobile with this entry, is mainly used to transmit data packets to any other node in the network.

2.2.1.1 Protocol overview and functions

Each node in a MANET maintains local routing table mainly for transmitting data packets and also for creating connectivity to different nodes in the current network. Thus, a node lists all the currently available destination nodes, and the total number of hop count necessary to reach every destination node listed in its routing table. Each routing entry is typically marked with a sequence number that is initiated by the destination node. Each node in the network maintains consistency by broadcasting routing information periodically.

Thus, the routing table of each node reflects most recent information about the current network. The control packets being broadcasted to all neighbouring nodes indicate which nodes are currently accessible and the number of hops required to reach a particular node. The control packets may be broadcast with either data link layer address or network layer address (Perkins andBhagwat2000). Routing information in a MANET is advertised using either broadcasting or multicasting the data packets. This process is repeated periodically when the mobile nodes freely move within the current network. The DSDV protocol needs that each node in the current network must frequently advertise to all its neighbouring nodes about its routing table content. As the information in the routing table may change very rapidly, the advertisement process should also be made repeatedly to guarantee that every mobile node can locate its immediate neighbouring node in the network.

This agreement needs to ensure that the source node takes only the smallest number of intermediate hops through a route to the destination node. This mechanism is the only way for a node to exchange data packets if there is no direct communication link exists with the destination node. The broadcasting mechanism in MANETs which is initiated by a node will contain information as listed in Table 2.1.

Table 2.1 Important fields of data broadcast in MANETs

Broadcasting Information
1. Sequence Number stamped by the destination node
2. Destination Address
3. Hop count

The routing tables being transmitted will also include information like the network address and hardware address of the node broadcasting them. The sequence number which is generated by the transmitting node is chosen as the origin for formulating forwarding decision. The new updated sequence number may make a decision on how to sustain the routing information for that particular mobile node. The receiving node always increments the entry before transmission and then transmits it through broadcasting.

Broken links in MANETs can occur as the mobile nodes move from one place to another place rapidly. The Data link layer protocol is mainly used for this purpose which may be indicated as infinity. The broadcasting information described by the DSDV protocol belongs to either full dump or incremental dump. In case of full dump, control packets contain all necessary information about a route. On the other hand, incremental dump broadcasting will take the information that has varied from the time when last transmission occurred. Irrespective of the type of broadcasting scheme being applied, transmission is done through network protocol data units. A node in a

MANET accepts the incoming broadcasting information if and only if it is new (i.e., with updated larger sequence number).

Example

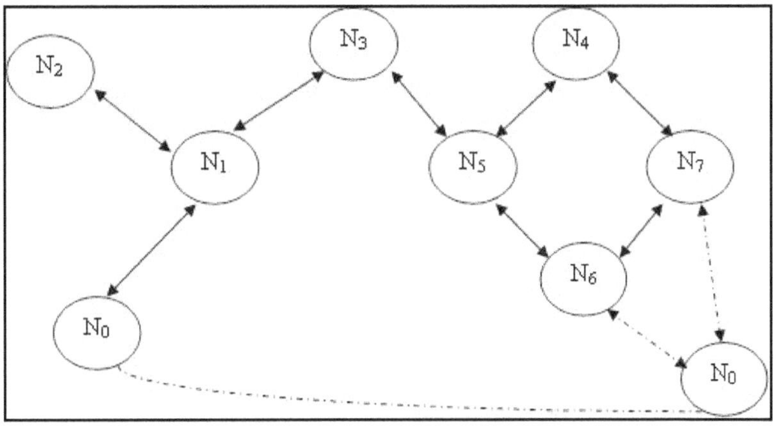

Figure 2.1 Node movements in a MANET

The Figure 2.1 has eight nodes in the current network. Consider the changes that can occurred in the routing table of N_3 node with respect to the mobility of N_0. In order to construct and manipulate initial entries of the routing table, each node broadcast its current routing information to all its neighbouring nodes. This process is repeated until all nodes update its routing table. Thus, the routing table of node N_0(He 2002) looks as listed in Table 2.2.

Table 2.2 Routing table entries at N_3

Destination node	Next hop	Metric	Sequence Number	Stable Information
N_0	N_1	2	S305_N_0	Ptr1_N_0
N_1	N_1	1	S105_N_1	Ptr1_N_1
N_2	N_1	2	S446_N_2	Ptr1_N_2
N_3	N_3	0	S601_N_3	Ptr1_N_3
N_4	N_5	2	S229_N_4	Ptr1_N_4
N_5	N_5	1	S065_N_5	Ptr1_N_5
N_6	N_5	2	S105_N_6	Ptr1_N_6
N_7	N_5	3	S045_N_7	Ptr1_N_7

After a particular period of time, node $N3$ forwards its routing table which would be as depicted in Table 2.3.

Table 2.3 Entries in forwarding table of node N_4

Destination node	Metric	Sequence Number
N_0	2	S305_N_0
N_1	1	S105_N_1
N_2	2	S446_N_2
N_3	0	S601_N_3
N_4	2	S229_N_4
N_5	1	S065_N_5
N_6	2	S105_N_6
N_7	3	S045_N_7

When the node N_0 moves from its current location as shown in Figure 2.1 closer to N_6 and N_7 then the communication link between N_0 and N_1 will not be working. As a result, the metric entry at N_1 for N_0 is assigned as infinity and also changed the sequence number to odd in the routing table of node N_2. In order to reflect these changes, node N_2 forwards its routing table to all neighbouring nodes. In this process, nodeN_3 will accept its current routing information. Discovery and choice of a particular route always depends on smaller hop count if and only if the value of sequence number reflects the same. After node N_0 moved to new location, the routing table looks as depicted in Table 2.4.

Table 2.4 Routing table entries after N_0 movement

Destination node	Next hop	Metric	Sequence Number	Stable Information
N_0	N_5	3	S417_N_0	Ptr1_N_0
N_1	N_1	1	S383_N_1	Ptr1_N_1
N_2	N_1	2	S561_N_2	Ptr1_N_2
N_3	N_3	0	S720_N_3	Ptr1_N_3
N_4	N_5	2	S347_N_4	Ptr1_N_4
N_5	N_5	1	S193_N_5	Ptr1_N_5
N_6	N_5	2	S354_N_6	Ptr1_N_6
N_7	N_5	3	S158_N_7	Ptr1_N_7

And, node N_3's forwarding table entries would be as depicted in Table 2.5.

Table 2.5 Forwarding table of node N_3

Destination node	Metric	Sequence Number
N_1	3	S417_N_0
N_1	1	S383_N_1
N_1	2	S561_N_2
N_1	0	S720_N_3
N_1	2	S347_N_4
N_1	1	S193_N_5
N_1	2	S354_N_6
N_1	3	S158_N_7

2.2.1.2 Limitations of DSDV Protocol

- It failed to support multicast routing.
- It is a tedious process of determining a delay time for advertising of routing information (Patel 2000).
- Unnecessary routing advertisement could waste network bandwidth even during stable network (Islam *et al.* 2012).

- Larger size routing table is required for a hug network which is difficult to sustain. Larger network might also increase overhead and requires more bandwidth.

2.2.2 Overview of DSR Protocol

The DSR protocol consists of two important mechanisms which work simultaneously to discover a new route and its maintenance in MANETs. The route discovery procedure is initiated by a source node wants to transmit a data packet to a target node, gains a route to the destination node. Route Discovery process is applied only when the source node attempts to transfer a data packet to the destination node and cannot have knowledge about the route to the destination node (Sharma *et al.* 2012).

Route Maintenance is the procedure by which a source node is able to discover using a source path to the destination node, if the network structure has distorted such that the source node cannot be able to use the pre-established route to the destination node because such link along the path no longer exists. When a route is broken, then a source node can try to use alternate route to reach the destination node, or can sometimes call upon route discovery procedure again to discover a fresh route (Chada*et al.* 2012).

Both route discovery procedure and route maintenance procedure works completely on demand. Unlike other routing protocols, the DSR protocol does not require periodic transmission of any kind of packets at any time within the current network. For example, the DSR protocol does not broadcast any control packets periodically like routing announcement, link status, etc(Shrivastava*et al.* 2011).

2.2.2.1 Limitations of DSR protocol

- The route maintenance procedure won't help to renovate a broken communication link.
- The old route descriptive information stored in the local cache could result in contradiction while reforming the route.
- The connection setup time is more than in other table-driven routing protocols.
- The DSR protocol degrades performance as mobility of nodes increase rapidly.
- The source routing procedure exercised by the DSR protocol substantially increases routing overhead. This overhead is directly proportional to the length of the communication path.

2.2.3 Temporally Ordered Routing Protocol (TORP)

TORP is suitable for multi hop based networks and relies on on-demand basis. TORP belongs to source-initiated routing scheme which performs better in highly dynamic based multi-hop networks (Pragati andNath, 2012). As soon as the source mobile node wants to transmit data packets, TORP initiates route discovery to find a suitable path by localizing routing changes, thus minimizing the communication overhead to certain extent (Kuppusamy*et al.* 2011). In order to discover the shortest path from a source mobile node to a particular destination node, TORP selects the right direction to next suitable intermediate destination to forward data packets. The source mobile node always keeps information about downstream path in the form of directed graph which does not contain loops to a destination mobile node using multiple hops.

TORP fundamentally performs three important tasks:

i. Establishment of a new path from source mobile node to a destination mobile node.
ii. Maintenance of the path
iii. Eliminating the pre-established path, if it is no longer suitable.

2.2.3.1 Limitations of TORP

- TORP performs similar to other on-demand
- TORP is not widely used as both AODV and DSR outperforms TORP.
- TORP does not support scalability.

2.2.4 Optimized Link State Routing Protocol (OLSRP)

Optimized Link State Routing Protocol (OLSRP) belongs to proactive routing protocol for MANETs. OLSRP inherits features from link state protocol and has benefit of providing routes immediately when required. All nodes maintain a table of routing information to every other node in the current network.

OLSRP is an advanced version of classical link state algorithm. OLSRP employs the idea of Multi Point Relays (MPR) to minimize the overhead caused by flooding the control packets in the network. This is achieved by only transmitting selected retransmission of control packets. OLSRP applies two different control messages like Hello (H) and Topology Control (TC) in the network. The former type of messages is mainly applied to determine either the link state information or neighbouring nodes. The latter type of message is used to advertise own information to neighbouring nodes which includes the MPR list (Finn 1987). OLSRP protocol is well suited for dense and large networks and works entirely in distributed nature and does not rely on any central controller.

Each node in the network floods control packets periodically and can be able to recognize the loss of such packets; thus OLSRP does not require reliable data transmission. In addition, OLSRP does not require delivering messages in sequence order at the destination node. Each message contains a different sequence number which is linearly incremented for each message. Thus, the destination node can recognize the most recent message, even if the received messages are out of order.

2.2.4.1 Limitations of OLSRP

- OLSRP preserves routing table for all existing routes; thus increases the need for more extra storage.
- The control overhead increases with the increase in the number of nodes.
- In order to rediscover a broken link, OLSRP consumes additional time.
- Discovering an alternative route enables OLSRP protocol to consume more power.

2.2.5 Geographic Routing Protocol

Geographic Routing Protocol (GRP) is a location based protocol in which each node can reach a destination node based on coordinate values. Thus, a node can never reach another node in the network without knowing its current location. Therefore, geographic routing algorithm must be improved to offer a service which can map identifiers of a node and its locations. The global positioning system avoids this problem to support a larger network without scalability issue. When a mobile node changes its current location then it can be informed by flooding hello packets. There is no need for exchanging and maintaining any routing information locally; thus works as stateless.

This characteristic makes geographic based routing algorithms attractive for MANETs and sensor networks. Largely many geographic based routing algorithms follow greedy approach for selecting a neighbouring node which is closest to a destination node as the next immediate hop (HouandLi1986). Geographic based routing algorithm delivers a message to a specific node in an ad-hoc network through multiple hops using positioning information. The process of discovering a route does not rely either on network address of a node or its routing table; instead, routing messages towards the location of a destination node.

2.2.5.1 Limitations of GRP

- Obtaining and preserving information about a specific route is very expensive as it requires additional message broadcast operations which require bandwidth, energy, and frequent updates.
- The state requirement of GRP is proportional to the number of its neighbours
- The traffics and states of all intermediate route cache of GRP increase as the number of paths and path length increase.

The taxonomy of the traditional routing protocols with their important properties, features and limitations are given in Table 2.6.

Table 2.6 Taxonomy of various traditional routing protocols

Protocol Name	Route Acquisition	Flooding for Route detection	Multipath Capability	Upon Link Failure	Storage Requirement	Power and Energy Conservation
DSDV	Computed based on a priori.	Do not use flooding to discover a new route.	Do not support	Flooding route update message to all intermediate nodes.	Low	No
DSR	Establish a route only when required.	Used cashing to minimize flooding.	Salvaging technique may be applied to restore a broken route	Route error message notified to the source node to remove invalid route.	Partial	No
AODV	Establish a route only when required.	Conventional utilization of caching to reduce flooding.	Do not support	Link error messages broadcasted to remove invalid path.	Partial	No
GRP	Based on location of a node.	Exchanges hello messages.	Provides Support	Flooding messages to discover an alternate path.	Stateless	No

2.3 MULTICAST ROUTE DISCOVERY PROTOCOLS IN MANETS

This section briefly discusses a few existing routing protocols that support multicasting in MNAETs. The existing protocols are discussed on three different categories of their operation executed on three different layers: the application layer, the IP (network) layer, and the MAC layer.

2.3.1 Application Layer based Multicast Routing Protocols

Application layer based routing protocol constructs a virtual communication infrastructure to setup an overlay network which sits on top of another network (i.e., physical network). Each link in such network represents a unicast communication channel in the overlay network which is not widely deployed (BiswasandNandy, 2004,JetchevaandJohnson 2001,SinhaandBharghavan 1999, Lee *et al.* 2002 andKim andKim 2005).

2.3.1.1 Ad Hoc multicast routing protocol

Ad Hoc Multicast Routing Protocol (AMRP) (JetchevaandJohnson2001) constructs bidirectional multicast routes from a source node to the members of a multicast group in the form of shared tree by using unicast communication channel. A logical hub in each group is responsible for the maintenance of group members and the tree. Initially, each member in a group declares itself as the logical hub with size one and frequently floods REQ control packet to determine other disjoint segments of the group. When a member of the group receives REQ packet from the hub from the disjoint segment but from the same group, it creates a new bidirectional communication tunnel and replies by sending JACK control packet. A member which is either hub or non-hub responds to the JACK packet to circumvent many communication links to the hub. According to

AMRP, only one member can become the core hub to create the mesh. After words, the core hub frequently broadcasts TREECREATE packet to all neighbour nodes to create shared tree. If a node receives a second copy of TREECREATE packet then it sends back TREE-CREATE-NAK packet through the same link.Thus it is marked as mesh link. Any node which wants to leave a group can forward JNAK packet only to all its neighbours.

2.3.1.2 Progressively adapted sub-tree for dynamic mesh

Progressively Adapted Sub-tree for Dynamic Mesh (PASDM) (SinhaandBharghavan 1999) is a type of overlay multicasting protocol which is capable of constructing a virtual based mesh spanning using all the members of a group. PASDM uses unicast routing along with forwarding mechanism to achieve multicasting functionality. A multicasting session may begin by creating a virtual based mesh and spanning all members of the group. A node in the multicast groups can discover its immediate neighbour by flooding the ERS approach (Sun *et al.* 2003).For achieving this goal, each node can exchange Group-REQ packets among all its neighbouring nodes. When node A obtains a GROUP-REQ packet from node B, it marks node B as its immediate neighbour in its mesh and the distance to reach node B and also records this information. A node in a group stops the neighbour detection process when the count of virtual Neighbouring nodes of that node attains the threshold value. When a node cannot able to locate its immediate neighbour using ERS approach then it can use flooding technique to discover neighbours.

Each source node creates its individual data packet delivery tree using the entries in its local link table. For this purpose, each node uses the source based steiner rules which permit the source node to create a steiner tree(Zhang *et al.* 2017) based on the value of adaptive cost,i.e.,the smallest adaptive cost is selected. A source node constructs a tree by considering all its immediate Neighbouring nodes as children and partitions the outstanding nodes as a subgroup. Instead of computing the entire multicast tree, the source node keeps each subgroup information into the packet header and combines it with the data packet and unicast it to the respective children. Then it is the responsibility of the children to forward the received packet to all members of the group.

When a new node wants to join a multicast group then it uses the usual neighbour detection procedure. A member of the anticipated group responds with GROUP-REP control packet. Then, the node gathers information about its individual virtual neighbours to setup its personal link state. To leave a group, a node cans unicast a GROUP-IV control packet to all its current neighbouring nodes.

2.3.1.3 Application layer multicast protocol

Application Layer Multicast Protocol (ALMP) (BiswasandNandy 2004) constructs a logical link based multicast tree using all the members of a group in a decentralized, incremental and dynamic way. ALMP detects and manage each node's mobility by measuring the Round Trip Time (RTT). When the RTT value of the parent exceeds the pre-set threshold value then a node should execute a reconfiguration process on its own delivery tree. An edge in this tree reflects the logical link between two nodes. Each member of a group discover its parent node by itself, once detected and links, it can assist one or any number of children. Whenever a node collects a data packet from its source node, it formulates many redundant copies of the data packet and sends a replica to every child nodes. If the performance degrades below a user defined threshold value, a member node either changing its current parent node or releasing its child nodes and also reconfigures the tree locally. A new node can join a group by sending join control message to all existing members of that group. Similarly, a node can leave a group at any time by sending leave control message to all its child nodes and also to its parent. Thus, the parent node will remove the node from its own list of child nodes.

2.3.1.4 On-demand overlay multicast algorithm

On-demand Overlay Multicast Algorithm (OOMA) (Lee *et al.* 2002) belongs to reactive type of protocol that generates an overlay using all the members of a group on demand. An overlay constructed is a source node rooted tree that links all members of a group using IP-in-IP encapsulation and tunnelling mechanism.

When a source node sends a multicasting packet and does not receive overlay packet for the multicasting packet then the source node buffers the packet locally and broadcast JREQ packet to all its Neighbouring nodes to create overlay. The neighbour node that is a member of the group which receives JREQ packet keeps the current member for this particular group (i.e., upstream member). The node also marks the JREQ of the current member as its personal address and disconnects the last member field. Afterwards, the node unicast the JREP control packet to all its upstream nodes and instantaneously forwards the control packet as the disconnected entry is zero. Any non-member of a group receives non-duplicate of the JREQ packet then the value of the disconnected last member field is incremented by one. The same process is repeated until the complete source tree is created. A link failure can occur when a node leaves a group. The link failure will be corrected during the recreation of the overlay next time. The taxonomy of the application layer based multicasting protocols with their few important properties, features and limitations are given in Table 2.7.

Table 2.7 Taxonomy of Application Layer based Multicasting protocols

Protocol	Efficiency	Robustness	Scalability	Network Topology	Limitations
AMRP	Efficient	Robust	Not scalable	• Support virtual mesh based topology • Multicast tree	• Loop formation • No-optimal trees • Higher overhead • Single point of failure
PASDM	• Efficiency depends on the use of physical links using unicast channels	Not Robust	Scalable	• Virtual mesh topology	• Redundant data transmission • Does not predict nodes mobility • Hide existent network topology
ALMP	Efficient	Simple to Deploy	Scalable	• Overlay multicast tree	• Causes control traffic overhead • Suffers from congestion
OOMA	Less Efficient	Not Robust	Scalable	• Overlay network • Source rooted tree	• Frequent link failure

2.4 NETWORK LAYER BASED ROUTING PROTOCOLS

2.4.1 Differential Destination based Multicast Protocol

Differential Description based Multicast Protocol (DDMP) (Chiang *et al.* 1998) relies on receiver-initiated scheme. DDMP typically works in two different modes of operation: soft-state mode and stateless mode. In former mode of operation, a source node includes the destination address into the data field of the packet and unicast the packet, to the next mobile node. A node receives such packet extract the address of the Neighbouring node and then unicast the same packet to the next node. This process is repeated until the intended destination node receives the data packet. This kind of unicast data forwarding method helps DDMP to avoid caching and maintaining the current state of a node and its address locally. The DDM protocol is well suitable for small type of dynamic multicast applications for MANETs.

2.4.2 Associativity based Ad Hoc Multicast Protocol

Associativity based Ad Hoc Multicast (AAM) protocol (Aceves and Madruga1999) is a source based on-demand multicast routing protocol which is well suited for Ad Hoc networks. AAM establishes a multicast tree at the source node for each session using association stability which permits the source node to discover a route to its intended destination node that requires minimal reconfiguration and stands longer time. In order to begin a multicasting session, a multicasting source node broadcasts/transmits a Multicasting Broadcast Query (MBQ) control packet in the current network. Each node receives the MBQ packet extract and record information like signal strength, address, power level, load in route relay and associativity ticks. A multicast receiver who wants to join in a multicast group can collect necessary information from the MBQ packet. A stable route for a multicast sender will be opt among all existing routes and the multicast sender replies by send the MBQ Reply packet using the same route.

A multicast sender may receive multiple copies of MBQ_Reply packets from multicast receivers. From the received packets the multicast sender constructs a stable multicasting tree and also generates aMC_Setup packet which will be broadcast to all nodes of the tree. When a node wants to leave a multicast group, then it sends Leave control packet and so the specific node will be pruned. A multicast tree may be deleted if a source node does not want to be an active multicasting sender.

2.4.3 Weighted Multicast Routing Protocol

Weight-based Multicast routing protocol (WMP) (JiandCorson2001) is a protocol in which transmission is initiated by the receiver. WMP relies on weighting factor when choosing the access point in the multicasting tree during a new entry in the group. When a receiver node wants to join a group, it floods a JREQ control packet with TTL entry. Such control packet is flooded until it reaches a node of the tree. After receiving the JREQ control packet, the tree node answers with a Reply control packet that contains information such as distance between pair of nodes: (source node, tree node), and (new receiver, tree node). When a node wants to join a group multicast group using an intermediate node then the hop distance from (destination node, source node) pair will be minimum.

The Joinweight factor attempts to discover the best path by taking into account the total number of forwarding nodes and the hop distance between the source node and the destination node. After receiving several Reply messages, the node preserves the best message. The best reply message lessens the quantity factor (q) = [(1-Joinweight) × (hop distance between the receiver node and a tree node-1)] + [(Joinweight × (hop distance between the receiver node and a tree node) + (hop distance between the tree node and the source node)].

2.4.4 Bandwidth Efficient Multicast

Bandwidth Efficient Multicast Protocol (BEMP) (Chiang *et al.* 1998) is focused on efficient utilization of network bandwidth by building a receiver initiated multicasting source tree. BEMP detects the closest member of a forwarding group by broadcasting Join message instead of discovering the shortest route between the source node and the receiver; thus controlling data transmission to certain extent. Every node on the route then turns into forwarding nodes. However, unnecessary forwarding nodes can be removed through optimization process which saves network bandwidth. If a node A desires to join a multicast group then it floods a Join control packet until it reaches either a receiver or forwarding node. A receiver or forwarding node hangs around till it reaches the predefined time or some number of Join control packets have been received. Reply control packet is sent to node A using the reverse route that the Join packets travelled.

When a node M wants to leave a group then it sends Quit control packet through its upstream. Once the Quit control packet has been received, the node in the upstream removes node M. BEMP applies Hard-state mechanism to preserve the network topology (Yang and Liao 2008).

2.4.5 Zone Routing Multicast Protocol

Zone Routing based Multicast Protocol (ZRMP) (Cai*et al.* 2006) is a receiver instigated multicasting based routing protocol. It extracts important features from proactive and reactive routing algorithms whereas a reactive algorithm has been applied across a zone and a proactive algorithm has been exercised inside the zone. Initially, a source mobile node creates a multicasting tree only for the inside transmission zone and then tries to extend it to the outside zone. A mobile node that wants to join in a multicast group typically changes its state from forwarding node to the member of the group. The taxonomy of the existing network layer based multicasting protocols with their properties, features and limitations are given in Table 2.8.

Table 2.8 Taxonomy of Network Layer based Multicasting protocols

Protocol	Efficiency	Robustness	Scalability	Network Topology	Limitations
DDMP	• Requires smallest amount of memory resources	No	Yes	• Uses unicast data transmission	• Requires considerable network bandwidth to broadcast Join control packets
AAM	• Achieved high data packet delivery	No	No	• Multicast based Tree topology	• Latency is high
WMP	• Efficient • Achieved high data packet delivery	Path loss is minimal	No	• Graph based network topology	• Suffers from network load and size of the multicast group
BEMP	• Saves network bandwidth	Yes	Yes	• Multicast based Tree topology	• Requires larger resource • Takes more time to deliver data packets to a destination
ZRMP	• Creates less control overhead than DDMP	Yes	Yes	• Zone based protocol	• Creates and maintains more states at an intermediate node

2.5 MACLAYER BASED ROUTING PROTOCOLS

Quite a few algorithms have been proposed in the past to offer MAC layer service that carry out multicast communication in Ad Hoc networks. These algorithms are designed with the aim of offering efficient and reliable multicast communication at the MAC layer(Perkins andBhagwat1994,Tang andGerla2003, Si andLi2004,Gossain*et al.* 2004).

2.5.1 Multicast Routing protocols for MAC Layer

Perkins andBhagwat(1994) have proposed an efficient and improved MAC protocol that supports multicast based communication for ad-hoc network. They have designed the MAC multicasting protocol by optimizing the IEEE 802.11 Distributed Coordination Function protocol (DCF). DCF protocol can be applied with any type of multicast routing protocol and brought a few important modifications to implement it properly. These modifications are: the data packets and Request-to-Send (RTS), Clear-to-Send (CTS), and Acknowledgement (ACK) control packets. The RTS control packet is modified as an extension namely, RTSExt control packet that includes four multicast addresses to locate next hop immediate neighbouring nodes, a factor that maintains the size of the RTS frame within the predefined bound limit.

The CTS control packet is modified as an extension namely, CTSExt frame that includes the list of the receiving nodes (i.e., the nodes that send the CTS frame), which assist the sender to separate among several CTS received frames. Similarly, the ACK frame is also modified and called as ACKExt frame, which includes the receiver's request order determined using the position index value (the sender sets an positive integer value in the RTSExt control frame to separate among several CTSExt frames and also in the DATA control frame to separate among several ACKExt control frames) of its address, which is extracted from the DATA frame. In addition, the header field of the DATA packet is modified and renamed as DATAExt frame, which includes fields like addresses of all nodes, which received the CTS frame successfully.

Neighbouring nodes are clustered into dissimilar groups and then flooding multicast data transmission to four closest Neighbouring nodes at a time. The nodes whose address field consist of RTSExt and an element of the multicast route must be ready to reply the CTSExt control frames. If multiple CTSExt control frames are transmitted simultaneously, the receiver cannot be able to receive it in proper order. Therefore, the CTSExt frames are transmitted one by one with a predefined delay between two successive transmissions.

2.5.2 Batch Mode Multicast Protocol / Location Aware Multicast Protocol (BMMP / LAMP)

Si andLi(2004) have proposed two different protocols to offer a MAC layer based multicast routing that provides reliable data service. The first scheme was known as Batch mode Multicast based MAC Protocol (BMMP) that utilizes a polling mechanism (TobagiandKleinrock1975). In order to evade the collision caused by transmitting multiple CTS frames at the same time (TobagiandKleinrock1975), the broadcast of either RTS or CTS frame should be in sequential at the destination in BMMP. Similarly, to avoid collision due to broadcasting many ACK control frames, the transmitting node must poll each neighbouring nodes by transmitting a new Request to ACK (RAK) control packet. This procedure creates a significant overhead when transferring a DATA packet to a destination node. The second scheme, which was called as Location Aware Multicast Protocol (LAMP) attempts to shun the overhead caused by the BMMP by guessing the location of each node in the current network. This scheme assists the source node to poll a particular group of nodes based on guessing their current location.

2.5.3 Broadcast Medium Window MAC (BMWM)

A multicast protocol that offers reliable data service based on round robin scheme has been proposed in the past (Tang andGerla2003,Gossain*et al.* 2004). The interaction between Medium Access Control (MAC) and routing layer are used to address the congestion control multicast routing problem in wireless Ad Hoc networks. Broadcast Medium Window (BMW) MAC protocol has also been introduced, which provides robust delivery to broadcast packets at the MAC layer. It shows that although BMW is able to provide high reliability under low to medium network load, reliability dramatically degrades under high network load. It is possible to extend it to the wireless On-Demand Multicast Routing Protocol (ODMRP) to facilitate congestion control in Ad Hoc networks using BMWM to combat the poor performance during highly congested network conditions.

2.5.4 Reliable Multicast MAC Protocol (RMMP)

Tang andGerla(2001) discussed a Reliable Sender-initiated MAC (RSM) protocol that employs separate communication channels. In order to provide reliable data service, RSM protocol uses busy tone instead of sending CTS and ACK control packets for representing multicast traffics in the MAC layer. This scheme helps to reduce the control overhead of the physical layer. In addition, two different busy tones are used: Acknowledgment based Busy Tone (ABT) and Receiver side Busy Tone (RBT). The RBT tone is applied in the similar way as recommended to eliminate the hidden terminal problem (SinhamandBharghavan1999), and its application is also extended to support multiple receiver nodes, allowing every receiver node to set up the RBT tone when receiving data packets.

The RBT tone has better-quality than the RTS/CTS scheme to address the hidden terminal problem. This is because of two reasons: first, data reception at the destination node is always assured to be collision free which significantly minimizes the total number of data packets being retransmitted. Secondly, the RBT tone let off few nodes from retaining the net allocation vector variable required in the CTS and RTS scheme, thus abridging the protocol.

The ABT tone is exploited to accept the data frames (i.e., the destination node will send an ABT tone back to the source node after a data frame is precisely received). The ABT tone which has been applied to achieve better performance has two advantages compared to using frames. First, the ABT tone does not require the support of header and physical layer preamble, thus ABT tone can be easily detected and an ABT tone does not produce either bit errors or collisions.

2.5.5 Multicast Sensitive MAC Protocol (MMP)

Tang andGerla(2000)presented a Multicast Sensitive MAC protocol (MSM) to support multicast traffics by appending an Extended Multicast Header that contains different information such as the next immediate hop which is believed to receive multicast packets. The idea of the multicast header is very similar to XCAST protocol header format, but the main difference between them is the representation of including the identifiers of the next immediate hops. MAC layer uses the extended header to offer reliable data delivery through an ACK scheme which will be transmitted from the source node to all other destination nodes using the identical multicast sub flow. Then, the transmitting node waits to receive the ACK packet from all of the destination nodes in a sequential order, thus evading the dispute between the source node and ACK packets. Retransmission of multicast packets which is performed using Multicast RTS (MRTS) and CTS is needed only if the source node never receives an ACK packet from any node. The taxonomy of the existing MAC layer based multicast routing protocols with their few important properties and limitations are given in Table 2.9.

2.6 ENERGY AND POWER EFFICIENT ROUTING PROTOCOLS FORMANET's

Rather than merely creating a suitable and efficient paths between a source node and a destination node, one of the most important design issue of a routing protocol being developed for MANETs is to extend either the network life time or functioning to certain extent. Efficiency can be achieved by minimizing power and energy of nodes in MANETs during data communication and also when nodes are in inactive state. There exist two different approaches to save nodes energy during active communication such as load distribution approach and transmission power control approach. In addition, scheme like sleep or power down mode mechanism is also available to keep nodes in inactive mode when they have no data to receive. There are many important energy associated metrics (Bourkerche*et al.* 2011) needs to considered to discover energy optimized or efficient route in MANETs such as: energy consumed, variance in a node's power level, time required to partition the underlying network, cost to be taken for transmitting a packet, and maximum cost of a node.

Table 2.9 Taxonomy of MAC Layer based Multicasting protocols

Protocol	Efficiency	Robustness	Scalability	Routing and Network Topology	Limitations
MMWP	Efficient	Yes	Yes	Used RTS, CTS and ACK packets for data transmission	• Significant overhead has been caused • Need a clustering algorithm if the number of next hop is greater than 4.
BMMP / LAMP	Waste network bandwidth, so not efficient	No	No	Uses RTS, CTS, ACK and RAK control packets for transmitting a single packet	• Creates higher control overhead when traffic is more. • Performs poor in dense network.
BMWM	Inefficient	No	No	Uses RTS and CTS control packets in round robin scheme	• More buffer size is required at an intermediate node • Length of RTS a packet causes communication overhead
RMMP	Acceptable level	No	Yes	Uses tones instead of RTS and CTS.	• Busy tones increase hardware complexity Performs poorly in dense network
MMP	Acceptable level	No	No	Relies on extender header, MRTS and CTS.	• Size of RTS frame causes more collisions • Believes intermediate node for reliable data service

The first parameter is very useful to offer the minimum-power-req path in which the energy consumption to deliver a data packet is largely minimized. In this mechanism, each link between two nodes is associated with a link cost which is represented in terms of transmission power being required and minimum-power-req is a route whose sum of the link cost of the path is minimum. However, a node requires more energy and power when it has more packet relaying functions to perform and also disturb the functionality of the entire network. Therefore, either maximizing or extending the life time of underlying network is a very important issue of an energy and power efficient route detection algorithm, i.e., among many existing routing paths, determining the one which will improve the network life time.

Typically, estimating the expected network life span is almost very difficult. Thus, the remaining three metrics aforementioned have been suggested to attain the ultimate goal indirectly.

The variation in the energy level of a node can be used as a sign of energy and power balance which can be mainly utilized to measure and extend the life time of an ad-hoc network. The cost-node-packet parameter indicates a node's battery life time in addition to energy level of a node. An energy conscious routing protocol should always prefer a wireless link that requires minimal transmission energy. In this scheme, the routing protocol must avoid a node whose energy level is presently low. Similarly, the energy efficient protocol to be proposed must select an intermediate node with maximum residual energy for packet forwarding.

2.6.1 Transmission Power-Control Approach

A routing scheme in a MANET fundamentally involves discovering an optimal path in an Ad Hoc network which can be modelled as a network graph, G=(V,E). In G, a vertex, V represents a node in the current network and an edge, E denotes a link between two nodes which falls in the same radio coverage area. When a mobile node wants to control its transmission power, then it should follow straight line communication with its intermediate neighbours and the total number of immediate neighbouring nodes should also be altered. It is always true that healthier transmission power enlarges the transmission coverage range and also minimizes the hop-count to a destination node.

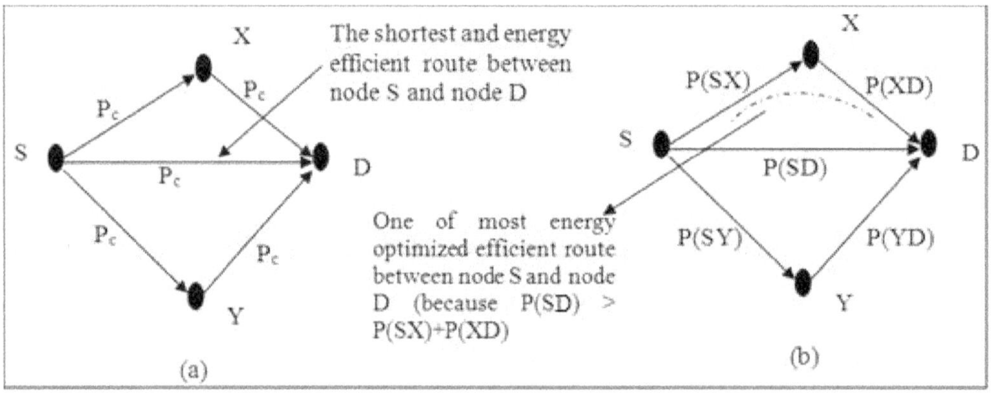

Figure 2.2 Two different power models: (a) Stable power model (b) Unpredictable power model

When a node's transmission power is stable,i.e., constant and not controllable as shown in Figure 2.2(a), the communication route P(SD) is the shortest path that takes most of the node's energy. On the opposite side, if a mobile node's transmission power is controllable,i.e., unpredictable, then it may take more energy to transmit data packets via intermediary nodes. This is because of transmission power required to communicate between two nodes has the most superlinear dependence on increase inthe distance from *d* to *d*2 (Perkins andBhagwat,2000).

Similarly, Figure 2.2(b) indicates that the communication route S→X→D is more energy optimized than the communication route S→D. The source node saves energy by taking minimal radio power to reach an intermediate node X, but not sufficient to arrive at the destination node D. On the other side, poor transmission power keeps a transmission to take larger hop count, thus increases the network partitioning time and communication delay time. For example, consider the benefits of adjusting or controlling the transmission power based on a node's power level as shown in Figure 2.2.

Topology creation, control and maintenance in a MANET by adjusting transmission power (RudolhandMeng1999, RamanathanandHain2000,Chang andTassiulas2000, Wattenhofer*et al.* 2001) is a challenging issue and still immature. Therefore, many researchers focused on providing a solution with the objective of maintaining a connected network topology, which takes minimal power. Designing an energy saving routing protocol for MANETs to discover the best route which diminishes the entire transmission power on the route between a source node and its destination is important.

It is very similar to optimization of a graph problem in which each edge is associated with a link cost that corresponds to the necessary transmission power (for example, P(SX) for the communication link S→A). Discovering an energy-efficient or optimal (minimum-power-required) route from node S to node D is equivalent to determining the least-cost route in the given weighted graph.

2.6.2 Transmission Power-Saving Protocols

This subsection briefly describes some existing transmission power saving approaches for MANETs. As each node in a MANET runs the route discovery algorithm, consistently the network graph optimization mechanism must be provided with vital information like the transmission energy of a node over the existing wireless link and also a node's residual energy.

Flow Augmentation Routing (FAR) protocol (Li *et al.* 2001) relies on the assumption that the total link costs along the optimal route between a source node and destination is always minimum. In this scheme, cost of each link is determined by using the cost of energy for each transmission, residual energy of a node, and weighing factors. A link that requires a smaller amount of transmission power and energy is chosen. Simultaneously, a broadcasting node that keeps higher residual energy directs to healthier energy stability. FAR protocol determines the optimal solution by applying operations in an iterative method. First, the FAR protocol solves the optimal path, then updates a node's link cost and residual energy, and repeats these steps till an optimal route will be discovered.

The FAR protocol extends the network lifetime only when data production rate is recognized in advance. The Online Maximum Minimum Routing (OMMR) (StojmenovicandLin, 2001) protocol attains the same objective with no knowledge of data production rate well in advance. In order to attain its ultimate goal, the OMMR protocol optimizes two important metrics of the MANET: maximize the minimal remaining power of a node (max-min problem) and minimize the power consumption of a node (min-power problem). The first metric is very helpful in avoiding the amount of overload caused by a node. The OMMR protocol first determines the optimal route between a known source node and its destination node by applying the single-source-shortest path algorithm based on the extracted link costs.

The identified min-power route always takes minimal power. In addition, the OMMR protocol attains multiple close-to-optimal with min-power route, which does not always diverge a lot from the optimal value and opts the best route that optimizes the max-min parameter.

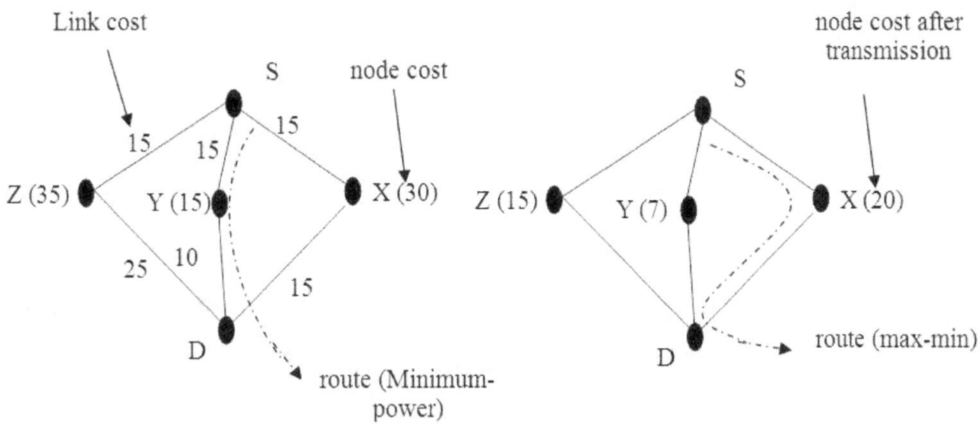

Figure 2.3 Different power enabled links of OMMR protocol. (a) Minimum-power route; (b) Min-max route

Figure 2.3 illustrates the operations performed by the OMMR protocol. In Figure 2.3(a), S→Y→D indicates the minimum-power required route because this path takes only minimal energy (Powermin = 25). Besides, the other two alternative routes S→X→D (route cost=30) and S→Z→D (route cost=40) can be considered for data transmission. In order to acquire the solution for max-min route among the existing three possible routes, the minimum power in each route must be compared. As each route in Figure 2.2(a) has one intermediate mobile node and thus the remaining energies of node X, Y and Z are compared. Finally, the path with minimum powered is selected. Similarly, the nodes X and Y in Figure 2.3(b) will contain the remaining energy of 20 and 7, respectively. Therefore, the best solution to the max-min route problem among the existing three routes is S→X→D.

Power aware Localized Routing Protocol (PLRP)(Doshi*et al.* 2002) relies on comprehensive information like power level or data generation information of each node in a MANET. It is practically very difficult to implement such scheme in real-time, because each mobile node in a MANET is usually provided with information only about its immediate Neighbouring nodes (i.e., local information). The PLRP protocol assumes that each sending node maintains local information about all its immediate Neighbouring nodes and also the destination node. It is very similar to aware of link costs (i.e., transmission energy) from each node to all its neighbour nodes and also to the destination node. This information is not sufficient to the source to discover an optimal route but detects the next immediate node through which the total transmission power required to reach the destination node is minimum. PLRP is a localized and distributed energy aware routing protocol.

The transmission power saving approaches requires power information like, the node cost and link cost. In order to estimate the information like node cost and link cost, the following problems need to be resolved. (a) Method to obtain precise information about power level of a node (b) Overhead caused during discovery of energy sensitive routing path and (c) Technique to maintain a route with minimum energy during mobility. The Reviewing Minimum Energy Routing (MER) protocol (Johnson andMaltz1996), overcomes the aforementioned by integrating power control tuning schemes in DSR (Woesner*et al.* 1998) and MAC protocol (Heinzelman*et al.* 2002) with eight different modifications as showninTable 2.10.

The power information is temporarily stored at all intermediate nodes towards the destination node and the destination node notifies the source node through route-reply control packet. Whenever the source nodes want to communicate with the destination node, it appends the power information in the packer header field, thus the routing path might use minimal power for successful transmission. The same process is also applied for transmission of MAC layer ACK control packets.

Table 2.10 Modification adopted in MERP

Modifications		Comment
i:	Routing packets based on power control	Software
ii:	Low energy routing path	Firmware
iii:	Cache replies off	Software
iv:	Internal cache timeout	Software
v:	Multi hops route establishment	Software
vi:	Transmission of ACK based on power control	Firmware
vii:	Route maintenance based on power sensing	Software
viii:	Mechanism of DATA/ACK snooping	Firmware

Options (ii), (iii) and (iv) are associated with route-cache mechanism of DSR routing protocol. Option (ii) is mainly used to determine the path with minimum power requirement. If the sender node has more routing paths to the same destination node, then by using option (i), the sender determines single optimal path. Option (vii) adjusts the low energy routing paths when the necessary power level changes due to mobility of nodes. Options (iii) and (viii) permit a non-member node to snoop on transmission and inform the sender node and MAC layer about the energy efficiency of the route.

Heinzelman*et al.*(2002) presented an algorithm namely LEACH to discover an efficient routing path which requires low energy for MANETs. The LEACH algorithm is performed in many stages in which each stage consists of two important steps: a setting up step which represents the initial event of the step and an exploring step that represents the last task of the step. During the setting up stage, the underlying network forms the cluster which forms nodes with similar properties. After a steady state is reached, a cluster member forwards the data packet to the base station which is then responsible to forward the received packet to the destination. In order to elect the Cluster

Head (CH) node, the presented LEACH algorithm determines its probability of selection.

$$P_x(t) = \begin{cases} \dfrac{k}{N - K\left(r \bmod \dfrac{n}{k}\right)} & C_i(t) = 1 \\ 0 & C_i(t) = 0 \end{cases} \qquad (2.1)$$

A Cluster Member (CM) who wants to act as CHis assigned with probability 0 and the probability for other nodes is determined by Equation. Where, *N* denotes the total numbers of nodes reside in the current network, k refers the total number of clusters formed and r represents the total number of rounds performed. In addition $C_i(t)$ denotes the CH node that wants to perform.

Any CM node who wants to transmit data during its own time window usesTDMA scheme. All other times, the CM nodes sit idle; thus energy is saved and life time of the current network is extended. However, we found two critical issues: first, as the CH node is responsible to forward a data packet received from a member node, it should always be awake. Second, sometime the CHs, which reside outside transmission area require more energy.The traditional routing protocol, AODV performs better when the time required to set up a MANET is small (YounisandFahmy2004). One of the noted features of AODV is offering better packet deliveryratio compared to DSR protocol. There exist different energy optimalroute discovery mechanisms for MANETs (Doshi*et al.* 2002,JohnsoonandMaltz1996). Specifically, the distinguished character for the classification is the time for performing optimization process. A mobile node in a MANET not only consumes energy when sending or transmitting data packets but also listens to the medium. Therefore, researchers focused on minimizing energy of a node wither during active transmission process or inactive listening period in MANET.

The algorithm presented by Kim and Lee (2008) namely, the Energy Efficient Hybrid Distributed (EEHD) algorithm relies on the density of the current network to offer energy efficient data transmission. The CHnode is selected based on its probability in using the energy level of the other nodes. The probability of selection of the CH node is calculated using the Equation (2.2).

$$CH_P = C_P \times \frac{E_{residual}}{E_{max}} \tag{2.2}$$

whereC_P denotes the constant value of the probability, $E_{residual}$ represents the residual energy of node, and E_{max} refers to the maximum energy level of the node. In EEHD algorithm, the cluster members nodes select the CH node using the probability and calculates the minimum reachability power required for transmission using the the following equation.

$$R = \frac{\sum_{i=1}^{n} MinPow_i}{M} \tag{2.3}$$

where$MinPow_i$ refers to the minimal energy required when i^{th}cluster member sends data to the CH node and M denotes the total number of CMs reside in its transmission range. Any node that becomes a CH node should have minimal reachability power value. At time t, any CM can compare its R value against R value of the current CH node and may become the CH node if its R value is small.

The Dynamic Multicast Routing (DMR) Algorithm discussed in (Lee *et al.*2017) is suitable for inference network and relies on network changes. DMR algorithm establishes the communication path and more importantly manages the current network based on clustering technique. In addition, DMR uses two step procedures to setup the routing path: Local discovery routing and flooding discovery routing. The former approach uses a step parent for setting and managing family of groups. The latter approach floods the message to all its immediate neighbour and repeats this process until a complete path is established.

The Lowest Identification Clustering (LIC) forms a cluster (with CH and CM) using the unique id value of each node in the network. The CH node is selected with lowest id value and compares its id value against each CM node. If a node's id value is greater than the id value of the CH node, then it becomes the CM. Sometimes a node may reside within the transmission range of two CH nodes, and then routing is performed with the help of gateway nodes. However, such a communication path may often disconnect and consumes more energy. The mobility based metric clustering algorithm (MOBICA) (BaldoandZorzi2008) is designed to form clusters based on speed of the CH node in MANETs.

To form a cluster, MOBICA uses the interval time for transmitting a hello message and speed of a node which is inferred using its coordination values. The node with low speed is then selected as the CH node. Afterwards, the CH node permits other nodes to become its CM. Even though the performance of MOBICA is better, communication between two nodes is disconnected and the network structure changes often.

An energy efficient scheduling algorithm namely, E-COPS (Basu*et al.* 2001) relies on establishing shortest optimal route between the source node and the destination node using multiple hops, if necessary. The shortest energy optimal path is selected based on relative angle of a node. Though E-COPS performs better than LIC algorithm and MOBIC algorithm, our proposed OTP algorithm selects an intermediate hop only if it's available energy is greater.

Shafighet *al.*(2012) proposed a mesh-based multicast route finding protocol that relies on fuzzy logics for MANETs. This algorithm handles imperfect information of ODMRP which is collected during route selection and establishes a strong forward group that leads to higher stability delivery structure. It changes the join query control packet to get information about nodes and classifies weak and strong nodes. Based on the available network bandwidth, loss rate measured, node's moving speed and power level, Fuzzy inferencing system classifies strong nodes and small nodes. The strong node has properties like high power level, high network bandwidth availability, minimum packet loss rate and low moving speed. A strong forwarding set is framed by using strong nodes. Then, using probability estimation, strong nodes can cache packets and forward them to its neighbors. This method claims that it offers better packet delivery rate, reducing latency between nodes and power consumption.

NarayananandThottungal(2013) have proposed a cross-layer based unicast routing scheme using fuzzy based decision making system for MANETs. This protocol uses fuzzy logic system(1) to opt for a route in source and fuzzy system(2) logic rules in a destination to monitor data transmission. In order to choose the best route to a precise destination mobile node, the source node performs the fuzzy-based optimized path selection process using information such as battery power, distance, and bandwidth. The stability of a path is measured using the accessible battery power, quality of link and distance. Source node uses nine fuzzy rules to pick up a best path from two parameters. To adjust a data rate from the destination mobile node, it selects fuzzy logic system(2) and takes the parameters delay between nodes and packet loss rate. Destination node uses nine fuzzy rules to regulate the data/control packet transmission of the source node. This result minimizes the latency between nodes and also packet loss rate.

Prasad *et al.*(2011) has proposed fuzzy enhanced adaptive delay routing protocol to choose an optimal route to destination. All intermediate mobile nodes that appear in the forward link collect the information about the previous nodes bandwidth, speed, packet loss rate and power reception of ROUTE REQ packet. Every node in mesh network applies fuzzy logic to determine the nodes probability of caching and forwarding.Based on the determined probability values of store-forward information, intermediate node grades the nodes into low, medium and high probability and stores the information in ROUTE REQ packet. Then, the source mobile node selects the strong forwarding group. This method decreases the resource consumption of the network. It reduces the overhead, delay between communicating nodes and power consumption and also affects the Packet Delivery Ratio (PDR).

ShanthiandNachiappan(2012) discussed a routing protocol that uses fuzzy logic and multi constrains to discover an optimal path to destination in multicast routing using different metrics like network bandwidth, delay between nodes, and the total number of currently available intermediate nodes. In this approach, every node utilizes a set of fuzzy rules to solve multi metric problem. Using fuzzy rules, this protocol uses prediction mechanism to choose the most unchanging path which satisfies various qualities of service constraints with low fuzzy cost with high path stability. This proposed protocol improves delivery ofpacket rate and path success ratio with minimal delay.

Sujatha*et al.*(2015) presented a fuzzy logic system namely Stable Multipath Routing (SMP) for finding all stable routes in MANETs. The proposed protocol provides reliable and stable quality path between nodes. It uses two phases: first phase takes the network bandwidth, node mobility, node energy, and link quality and reputation index metrics to select optimal route. Then, fuzzy logics are applied to select efficient nodes from the network which is referred as candidate node having special properties. In second phase, it constructs routing backbone in which multiple routes can be set up between sources to destination node. This protocol provides more security, optimized packet delivery rate, and reduced packet drop and delay.

Basarkode*t al.*(2014) proposed stability based routing protocol which is an enhancement of an existing protocol (ODMRP) to provide stable connection to support real-time applications. This work utilizes the node's important parameters like link stability, delay and bandwidth during stable route detection for offering an efficient and low computational power. The suggested protocol claims of offering minimal packet overhead, delays between nodes and increase in the packet delivery rate and on-demand service.

Yufang*et al.* (2014) proposed a tree based routing protocol, MAODV. It creates multiple routes dynamically to the destination. Route discovery is mainly based on an RREQ and RREP. When a source entails a path to a group of hosts, then it must a RREQ broadcast packet that contains a join flag (RREQ-J) and destination address with multicast address. A member of the tree with recently established route to a specific destination mobile node answers by broadcasting RREP packet. The non-members of the tree then rebroadcast the RREQ control packet. Nodes on receiving the RREQ control message must update its multicast route table. The route table retains the information about its immediate next hop and sequence number to a particular source. This information is more importantly used to maintain the same route to the same source.

When the originating node receives same reply message multiple times, RREP while establishing a new route, then it prefers a path based on fresh sequence number/minimal hop count. Then, an activation message, MACT to the multicast group is sent to initiate the route from the source mobile node to the node that sends reply message. If the source does not collect a MACT control message after pre-set time period, then it broadcasts next RREQ-J message. After a specific number of unsuccessful attempts, the source becomes the Group Leader. The group leader then periodically broadcasts group hello, GPRH control messages to smooth maintenance of group connectivity.

2.6.3 Sleep and Power saving Approach

The ultimate aim of maintaining sleep and power-down modes in an ad-hoc network is to effectively save the inactive time of mobile nodes when they do not have data to receive. As almost all radio based hardware maintains a few low power modes, it is always advantageous either to keep the radio/node in sleep mode or switch-off to save energy. For example, by maintaining sleep mode, the WLAN-II based IEEE 802.11 requires 250mA for receiving data packets and 300mA for transmitting data packets, at the same time both consume 9mA when switched to sleep mode (Chen *et al.* 2001).

In order to enable each node in a MANET to receive either data or control packets properly, it is not advisable to keep all nodes in sleep mode to save maximum energy. One of the possible solutions is to implement master-slave method,i.e., elect a node as a master and all remaining nodes are slaves.

The master node is responsible to coordinate the data communication process and provides necessary services to slave nodes. Thus, each slave node in the group can sleep maximum time to save battery energy. However, each slave must wake up at regular intervals and makes communication with the master to discover whether it has information to receive. But, a slave can go to sleep mode again when it will not be addressed. A multi-hop based MANET would maintain two or more master nodes because one master node cannot provide service to the entire network. Figure 2.4 shows the master-slave network architecture, where mobile nodes, except master nodes, can save energy by putting their radio hardware into low power state.

The master-slave architecture as depicted in Figure 2.4(a) is built on symmetric model where each master has equal radio power and same coverage range as slaves. Figure 2.4(b) represents the asymmetric model where each master node can have longer coverage range. Although, this kind of network model has been keenly studied for various reasons such as simplifying the process of location management and interference reduction (Deering 1989), the difficulty of picking up suitable master node and preserving the master-slave structure under dynamic topological change is still immature and a challenging problem.

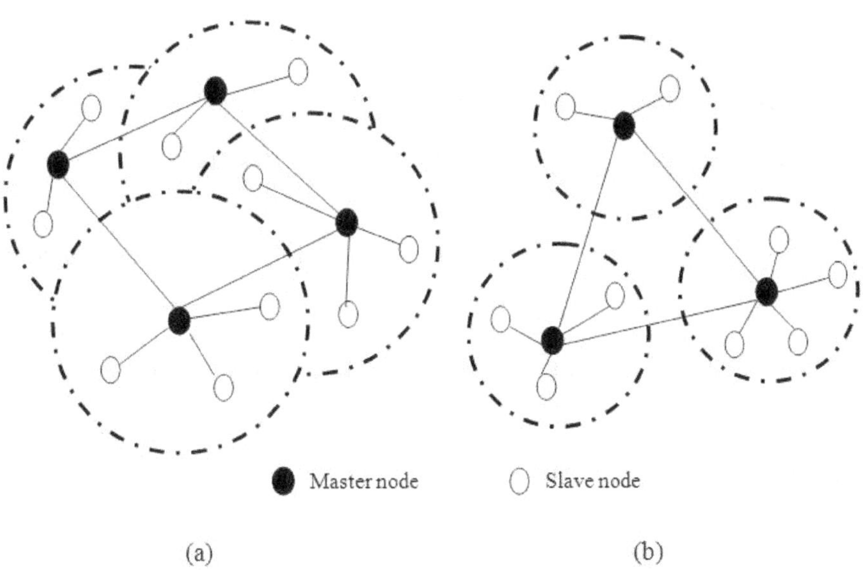

Figure 2.4 Master-Slave model in MANETs. (a) Symmetric model (b) Asymmetric model

In order to save energy, the Geographic Adaptive Fidelity (GAF) protocol (Girling*et al.* 1997) and SPAN protocol (Xu*et al.* 2001) work based on master-slave model and keep each slave node in low-power state whenever slave nodes don't have data to receive. Unlike GAF and SPAN, another protocol namely, Prototype Embedded Network (PEN) protocol (JubinandTornow1987) implements the sleep mode operation which is synchronized without relating any master node.

SPAN protocol (Xu*et al.* 2001) selects a master node dynamically by applying a distributed master eligibility rule where each node can freely and independently check if it can either turn out to be a master node or not. The rule states that if any two Neighbouring nodes cannot communicate each other directly or using one or more master nodes, then it can become the master node. By employing this rule, SPAN protocol provides healthy connectivity between master and slave nodes with significant energy savings. However, SPAN suffers two issues and they are as follows. First, the master nodes do not savetheminimal count and secondly each master node can be easily overloaded. In order to prevent these issues, each master node should periodically confirm whether it can continue as a master node or give chance to other nodes to turn out to be a new master. In addition, each slave node regularly finds out if there is a chance to become a new master or not.

In GAFP(Islam *et al.* 2012), each mobile node requires location information that relies on GPS technique to correlate it with an implicit cluster thus the entire current network area is separated into a few square clusters, and a node whose residual energy is high in each cluster turn out to be the master node of the cluster.

Whereas all the remaining mobile nodes in the cluster except the master node can be viewed as redundant nodes during broadcasting data packets and therefore they can safely switch to sleep mode without forfeit the network's routing efficiency. All slave nodes can switch between listening mode and sleep mode by guaranteeing that each master in each cluster will continue to awake the medium to transmit data packets.

Any node from cluster B,i.e., nodes b, c and d as shown in Figure 2.5 can broadcast data packets to node a, e and f; thus the remaining nodes can switch to sleep mode to save energy. The size of the cluster can be realized by using the correlation between the cluster size and the transmission coverage. The master selection rule works as follows. A node in a MANET can be in discovery, sleeping or active mode as depicted in Figure 2.6.

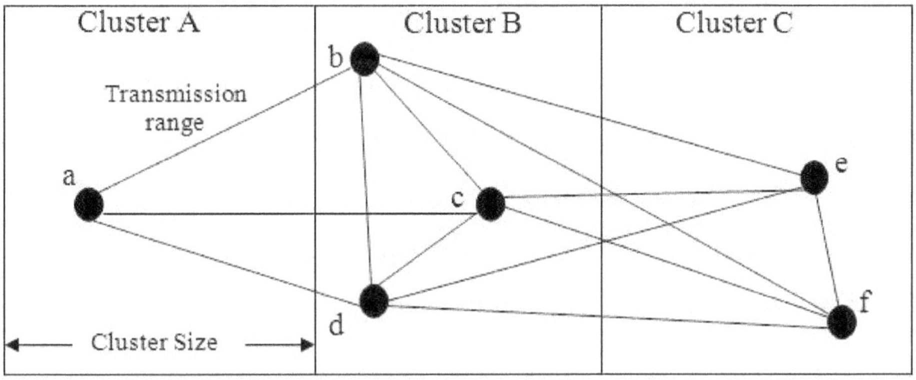

Figure 2.5 Virtual Cluster model of the GAFP

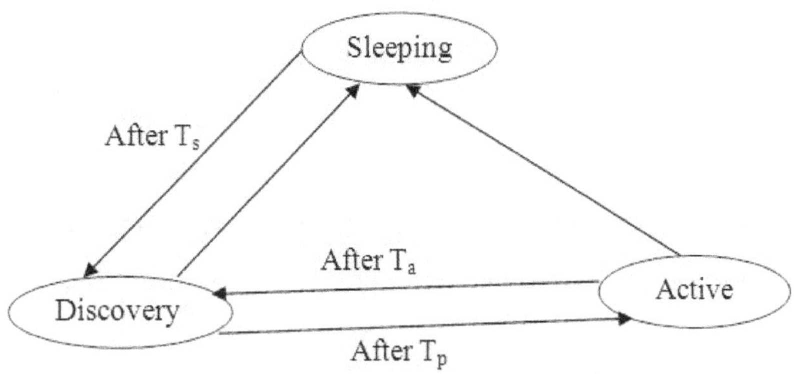

Figure 2.6 Power saving scheme in GAFP

In the beginning, a node can be in discovery mode and broadcast discovery messages along with its cluster ID to discover other hops within the cluster. A node may become a master node if such node does not receive discovery message after a predefined time interval T_p (Time required for entire processing) If more nodes stay in discovery state then the node with the highest anticipated duration becomes the master node. The master listens to the medium for the whole duration of T_a(time required in active state) to handle routing. Afterwards, the node may change its present state to offer a chance to the remaining nodes in the cluster to turn out to be a new master node. In a dynamically changing environment, each sleeping node should wake-up in advance to become a master and its sleeping time is determined by estimating the time of all the nodes that resides within the cluster.

Similar to GAF and SPAN, the PEN Protocol makes use of the communication functions that takes minimum-duty cycle and also power-off the node when stays in idle mode. Unlike GAF and SPAN, nodes within a cluster communicate 'asynchronously' excluding a master node and therefore, the master overcapacity issue can be evaded.

In anAd Hoc network, where there is no central device to provide all necessary service, each node in a cluster should periodically stay awake and listen to the medium, broadcast its presence by using *beacons* signals, and listen for a communication request control packet before switching to power-off state. A source node that wants to transmit data packets should wait until the source receives a *beacon* from the anticipated receiver node or server. Then, the source node informs its willingness to transfer data packets during which the medium is snooped and begins the communication process immediately.

Both route discovery and route upholding procedures have been applied in PEN protocol are very similar to the procedure applied in AODV (Perkins andRoyer1999) protocol, i.e., establishing a route only on-demand basis and exchanging routing table between Neighbouring nodes.

One of the noted features of the PEN protocol is taking minimal active time using its asynchronous functionality, and thus consumes significant energy. But the PEN protocol is useful when the interaction between nodes in a cluster is reasonably low and well suited for appliance concerning low command traffics. The taxonomy of the existing power and energy saving protocols for MANETs with their network topology with the observations and the limitations are tabulated and given in Table 2.11.

Table 2.11 Taxonomy of transmission power and energy control protocols

Protocol	Goal	Network Topology	Approach being applied	Observations/Limitations
FAR	Saving the energy during data transmission	Employs graph optimization using link cost	Saving the energy during active communication	Each node should have knowledge about data generation
OMMR	Saving the energy	Utilize graph optimization using min-max routes	Saving the energy during active communication	Assumes that the network traffic is evenly distributed when time intervene
PLRP	Saving the energy	Employs graph optimization using link cost	Saving the energy during active communication	Relies on using the global information about the current network
MER	Saving the energy	Control the required power during transmission to reach next node	Saving the energy during active communication	Utilized eight different options to address the issues found in DSR and IEEE MAC protocols
SPAN	Control energy consumption when a node is in inactivity	Adopts master-slave style for routing data	Reduce energy during inactivity using power-down/sleep modes	Master nodes in a network can be overloaded
GAFP	Control energy consumption	Uses GPS information and master-slave method	Reduce energy during inactivity using power	Sleeping time of a node depends on a node's stay time
PENP	Control energy consumption	Nodes can communicate asynchronously	Reduce energy during inactivity using power	Fails to support applications involving huge data traffics
SMP	Aims to save energy consumption during routing	Supports multi-hop routing	Apples fuzzy rules and node properties	Fails to discover shortest path
E-COPS	Saving the energy and power	Multi-hop based routing	Uses relative angle of each node to select shortest path	During, an intermediate node selection, it fails to determine whether a node is healthy or not

From the literature survey made for discovering a power and energy saving mechanism for MANETs, it is observed that the route discovery protocols or algorithms have been widely investigated by the researchers whereas only limited number of studies have been carried out for the route discovery with fuzzy logics and relative angle of a node.

In the recent days, energy and power optimization algorithms have been widely applied in many areas where instant infrastructure-less based network setup is required and the life time of MANETs plays a crucial role. A considerable amount of research work has been proposed by the researchers in the past for discovering shortest route between a source and a destination node that takes minimal power and energy, thus extending the lifetime of the current network is possible. Each existing solution or protocol suffers from at least anyone of the issues discussed above,andso fails to increase the network life time.

Even, many existing traditional routing protocols developed cannot be applied to a MANET to achieve the aforementioned goal. Because, in MANETs the node mobility, energy and power consumption, packet delivery rate, throughput, stability are crucial issues. Hence developing a new multicast routing algorithm or protocol to minimize energy and power consumption is very essential.

Hence, to address and overcome the issues found in the literature survey and to present the best multicast routing algorithm for MANETs, the following power and energy saving algorithms are to be developed.

(i) Developing a new multicast route discovery algorithm which establishes the shortest route between a source node and a destination node to get rid of the issues of the existing algorithms and provides optimal results than the existing algorithms reported in the thesis.

(ii) Devising a new cross-layer based multicast route discovery algorithm for MANETs aims to improve the life time of the current network.

2.7 SUMMARY

In this chapter, different categories of routing protocols like traditional routing protocols, energy and power efficient multicast routing protocols for MANETs are presented. The limitations of these protocols in each type and necessary of developing new cross-layer based multicast routing protocols for the improving throughput, stability, life-time, minimization of energy and power consumption of wireless nodes are also discussed.

CHAPTER 3

EXPLORATION OF OPTIMAL AND ENERGY EFFICIENT MULTICAST ROUTE DISCOVERY ALOGRITHM IN MANETS

As mobile nodes can freely move in and out of a MANET, its topology structure can also change over time, i.e., can't have fixed topological structure as wired networks. This causes many problems like link failure, redundant links, etc. This is because, only the source node initiates the route discovery process and solves the link failure issues by rerouting the data packets. Relay node sends only the route failure information to the source node. Introducing relay nodes to avoid link failure cannot be an ideal solution. Therefore, a novel algorithm to select Optimal Transmission Path (OTP) in a MANET has been proposed. The proposed OTP algorithm discovers an energy efficient route from source mobile node to the destination mobile node and also minimizes hop count and delay. This method mainly relies on the transmission- and receiving power of each node for efficient node selection in the current network.

3.1 PREAMBLE

A MANET is a cluster of wireless nodes forming an instant network. The formation of such a network has no wires, no centralized base station and infrastructure and even does not require administrative intervention (Winter *et al.* 2006). All nodes in a MANET have excellent sensing power, transmitting power and receiving power and can route packets to all its intermediate nodes in the network (Murthy and Manoj, 2004). Among various existing network architectures, a MANET has magnetized a lot of consideration in different real-time applications where wired network failed to setup. Typically, MANETs have no centralized device to control functions such as data transmission, forwarding, congestion control, etc. These constraints make routing the biggest challenge in MANET. In this environment, each node includes all function to forward data or control packets to the next immediate hop permitting them to reach the destination node through multiple hops.

Each node in the network may operate as router, source node, destination node and can move unreservedly in any direction and thus making rapid and irregular topology. The nodes in a MANET are often battery powered through a great assortment in their ability, thus conserving an individual node's power and energy is a crucial design problem and also becomes a challenging issue.

The nodes that recline within each other's communication range can communicate directly and also responsible for dynamically learning each other. However, to permit communication between nodes which do not fall within each other's radio coverage can use intermediate nodes. The important problems like energy consumption and transmission band become the root cause for node disconnection and rerouting. This problem can be resolved through multi-hop communication technique where source node can send data packets to its communicating node using intermediate nodes. However, a node requires more energy to communicate its destination node, which is located too far. The communication range is directly proportional to the energy requirement of a node. However, a MANET uses larger hop count to complete the data transmission.

Recently, implementing wireless based applications becomes a timely requirement and also very popular. There exist many routing discovery protocols for MANETs, which are proposed by researchers in the past. However, performance of a MANET becomes a crucial part of its design. This is because of its dynamic topological changes. Even, movement or disconnection of a single mobile node in a pre-established path increases route complexity problem, thereby affecting the performance of the whole network. Though, passive routing protocol like AODV handles node disconnectivity problem by implementing route discovery mechanism, restarting the same path many times causes problems like redundant paths and nodes. To address the aforementioned problems, we propose an Optimal Transmission Path (OTP) discovery algorithm to conserve power and energy of mobile nodes, thus lengthening the life time of the current network is possible. An intermediate node is selected by OTP algorithm based on its current energy level and relative angle.

3.2 PROPOSED OTP ALGORITHM

The main goal of this sub-phase of the research work is to develop an effective algorithm to select an optimal multicast routing algorithm in MANETs using energy level of each intermediate node from source to destination.

3.2.1 Working Principle of OTP Algorithm

The proposed OTP algorithm makes use of energy measurement equation modified first order ratio model (Chadha*et al.* 2012) by using equation (3.1) and modified optimal route selection algorithm (Shrivastava*et al.* 2011).

$$E_T(b,h) = E_{T-ep^2b}(b) + E_{T-amp}(b,h) \tag{3.1}$$

Where, $E_T(b, h)$ is the energy consumption while a source node transmits packet, h represents the distance between two nodes, which is measured in terms of hop counts, and b represents the data bits/packet.

The energy consumption is measured as the sum of E_{2} and $_{ep\ b}$

amp(b,h),i.e., the energy required for transmitting a single bit data by covering the distance 'h'. The energy consumption mainly depends on $E_{amp}(b, h)$ for covering distance 'h' than E_{T-ep^2b}(b).

In short, the factor 'h' between any two nodes becomes a crucial factor that decides the energy efficiency of the current network. The OTP algorithm mainly uses the energy and radio reception power of each node while selecting an intermediate node. Each node maintains different information as listed in Table 3.1.

Table 3.1 Packet information in a MANET

OTP
Packet Information
Source Destination Sequence number energy level Radio reception power Pre_hop Post_hop TTL

As each node maintains various important information such as transmit power level and radio reception power, selecting an optimal routing for data transmission, the lifetime of the current topology is increased rapidly. The proposed OTP algorithm works as described below.

i) First, the source node that desires to transmit data to its destination node selects an intermediate node based on relative angle and distance.

ii) The distance from the source node to the relay node decides the radio reception power of that node.

iii) To establish an optimal path, the source node chooses many intermediate healthy-powered nodes that increases the coverage distance.

The source node increases the transmission coverage area by checking whether an intermediate node is energy powered. The energy level of a node is measured using the equation (3.2).

$$RE = AE - [EC_T + EC_R) \tag{3.2}$$

where, AE represents the available energy of a node, EC_T and EC_R represent the energy consumed to complete data transmission and reception, respectively. If any intermediate node has residual energy greater than 90 percent, then that node is selected for discovering optimal path. Otherwise, the current node selects next immediate neighbour node based on its relative angle which is calculated using equation (3.3).

$$Inode^r_{ij} = \{0 < Inode^r_{ij} \leq \prod\} \tag{3.3}$$

Accordingly, the optimal path is established while a source node transmits a packet to the base station. The nodes of the established path leverage power and energy efficiency to increase the current topology life-time. The proposed OTP algorithm chooses suitable intermediate node based on relative angle as shown in Figure 3.1. In order to establish an energy efficient routing path, the OTP algorithm uses intermediate node which is located nearer to it (i.e., shorter distance, d) and largest relative angle (r). The underlying network cannot always maintain balanced transmission state.

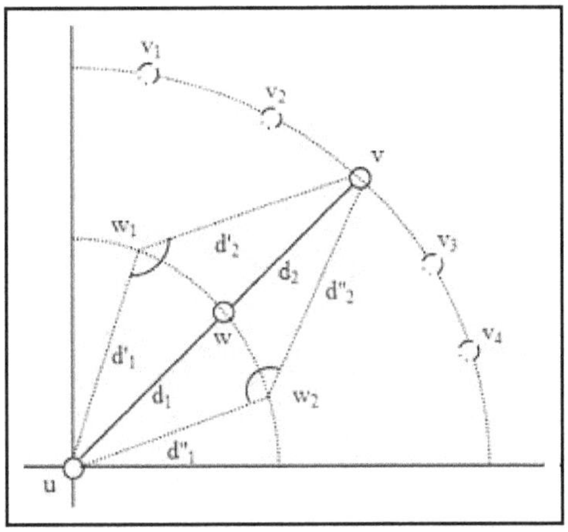

Figure 3.1 Selection of an intermediate node using OTP

When the data is being sent from source to destination through unbalanced distribution, the CH node needs to cover a larger distance to reach the base station; thus the energy conservation of CH node is increased. However, the proposed OTP algorithm increases current network life time by converting the unbalanced distribution into balanced distribution. Therefore, the energy conservation of each node is minimized during data transmission.

The OTP algorithm chooses the number of intermediate hops k, by balancing the distance between all its immediate Neighbouring nodes. The current routing path from the source node that wants to send data packets to the destination node must forward it to the base station is stated in Equation (3.4).

$$RP = \{CH_i, CH_{(i+1)}, \ldots, CH_{(i+k)}, i = 1\} \tag{3.4}$$

Where RP represents the temporary path established between the source node and the base station, CH denotes the cluster head node and k represents the number of intermediate hops. Table 3.3 depicts the algorithm for determining and selecting a power energized intermediate node. For understanding purpose, few notations have been listed in Table 3.2 with comment.

Table 3.2 Description of notations

Notation	Comment
r ← ø	Initially, optimal route path is empty
h	Healthiness of each intermediate node which is determined based on its energy and power
L	Length of the optimal route
E_{TS}	Energy of transceiver in sleep state
R←R ∪ h	Optimal route has been explored based on healthiness of the intermediate node

Table 3.3 Pseudo code to detect the first power energized intermediate node

Procedure: OTP Algorithm

```
Input: Source node (S) and Destination (d)
Output: Optimal route, r
begin
  r ← ø
  Inode^r_sd ← 0
  healthy h ← 0
  h[ ] ← intermediate nodes from S towards D
  n ← intermediate nodes h[ ] from S towards D
  L ← 0
  temp d^r_sd ← 0
R ← R ∪ S
while(L≤n) {
if ( Inode^r_sd > 0.9) then
        h ← h[L]
else {
Inode^r_sd ←determineangle(s,d)
if ( Inode^r_sd ≤ ∏/2)
d^r_sd ← root(d^2_sr + d^2_rd + 2d_sr d_rd cos(d^r_sd))
elseif ( Inode^r_sd > ∏/2)
        d^r_sd ← √(d^2_sr + d^2_rd − 2d_sr d_rd cos(d^r_sd))
        }
```

25	$h \leftarrow h[L]$ **end** $R \leftarrow R \cup h$
	end

Initially, the optimal route denoted empty set (ø). Based on the healthiness of each intermediate node from source to destination, the optimal route has been explored. If the RE of an intermediate node is greater than 50% then the transmitting node assumes that the selected intermediate node is not balanced. Thus, the source node increases the coverage area by adding more intermediate hops based on its relative angle.

As depicted in Table 3.3, to select an optimal energy efficient path/route, the source mobile node checks the power of the first intermediate mobile node. If the power of that node is high (greater than 90 percent), the source node extends its coverage distance with next node by applying the same procedure. When the energy is lower than the predefined value, then the source node determines its relative angle to discover an energy efficient intermediate node. This process is repeated until a stable and optimal path is discovered.

3.3 PERFORMANCEANALYSIS

In this section, we present the procedure for the simulation of proposed OTP algorithm using Network Simulator, NS2. The OTP algorithm is simulated in a scenario to evaluate its performance and efficiency in the network with different count of nodes that are installed randomly. The simulation is performed in wireless environment using the network size of $500*500m^2$. The performance of the OTP algorithm is compared with algorithms like MOBICA, LICA, and ECOPS. The various simulation parameters are tabulated in Table 3.4.

Table 3.4 Simulation parameters

Parameter	Value
Initial Energy	1 Joule
# Nodes	Between 30 and 50
Traffic Model	CBR
Simulation Area	500x500m^2
Transmission Range	250
Antenna Type	Omni Antenna
Network Interface Type	Wireless PHY
Channel Type	Wireless Channel

The performance of the OTP algorithm is validated based on different metrics: energy consumption, delay, packet loss ratio, packet delivery ratio and throughput. Figure 3.2 shows the portion of simulation network in which the current network comprises of several nodes which randomly appear in different locations and they can freely move in and out of the network. In addition, the central controller,i.e., base station pretends to be one of the nodes that appear in the middle.

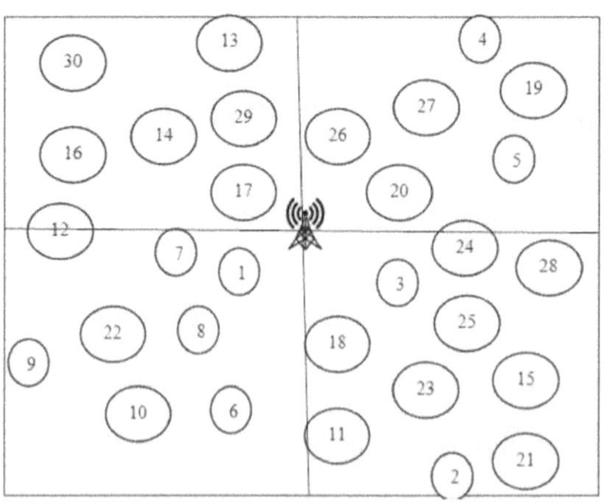

Figure 3.2 Portion of the network environment

When a CM wants to transmit data to the destination node then the CH node receives the data and forwards it to the BS, if and only if, the BS resides within the radio transmission range. When the BS resides outside the radio transmission range, then the CH uses multiple intermediate hops to reach the BS.

The performance of the proposed OTP algorithm is evaluated in two different simulation environments. First, the OTP algorithm is tested and analyzed by setting up flat network topology. The second simulation environment is focused on testing the OTP in a hierarchical network topology.

3.3.1 Simulation Environment 1 – Flat Network Topology

Different metrics like throughput, energy, packet delivery ratio, delay and packet loss ratio were used to analyze the performance of the proposed OTP and compared against existing protocols such as MOBICA, LIC, and E-COPS.

Each metric is simulated by using the same network environment against MOBICA, LIC, E-COPS and proposed OTP. And its recorded values are tabulated for analysis.

- **Packet Delivery Ratio**

The efficacy of a protocol can be measured by using its Packet Delivery Rate (PDR) across the entire network that is typically measured using total packets received from source to destination to total packet loss. Equation (3.5) is utilized to measure the PDR value.

$$PDR = \frac{\sum_{0}^{n} PktR(n)}{\sum_{0}^{n} PktR(n) + \sum_{0}^{n} PktL(n)} \tag{3.5}$$

where $\sum_{0}^{n}$PktR(n) -Total number of packets received

$\sum_{0}^{n}$PktL(n) -Total number of packets lost

Each protocol is simulated 10 times separately using NS2. The PDR caused by each of them including the proposed OTP algorithm have been recorded and its averaged values are plotted in a Table 3.5.

Table 3.5 PDR values of OTP, E-COPS, AGDA (Zeeshan*et al.* 2016) and FBORP (Sujatha*et al.* 2015)

Simulation Time (ms)	OTP	E-COPS	AGDA	FBORP
0	0	0	0	0
10	0.957	0.91	0.748	0.63
20	0.93	0.82	0.719	0.61
30	0.92	0.81	0.727	0.601
40	0.909	0.791	0.719	0.602
50	0.911	0.824	0.72	0.601
60	0.94	0.827	0.709	0.602
70	0.92	0.86	0.723	0.601
80	0.919	0.815	0.719	0.603
90	0.925	0.82	0.719	0.605
100	0.92	0.817	0.72	0.606

Different PDR values are generated against different simulation time which are expressed in milliseconds for OTP, E-COPS, AGDA, and FBORP are depicted in Figure 3.3.

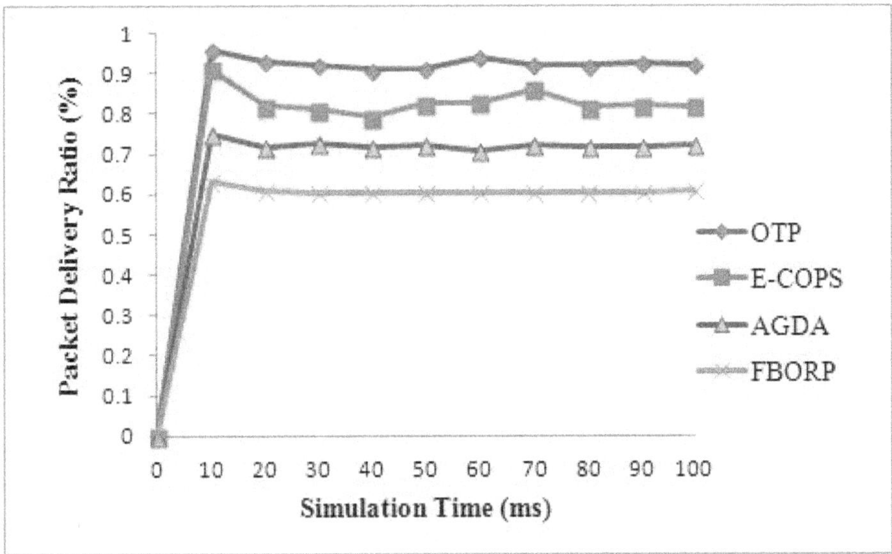

Figure 3.3 PDR of OTP, E-COPS, AGDA and FBORP – Case 1

The highest PDR value of OTP algorithm is 10%, 21.3% and 32.1 % greater than E-COPS, AGDA and FBORP routing protocols respectively. Figure 3.3 clearly points out that the proposed OTP improves the packet delivery ratio to certain level and outperforms than all other protocols.

- **Energy Consumption**

The amount of average remaining energy of a mobile node, while it is selected as an intermediate hop in a MANET is defined as the residual energy of that node. The energy consumption (i.e., the energy required for transmitting data packets) of a node is calculated by subtracting the residual energy from the total energy of that node. Table 3.6 and Figure 3.4 illustrate the Energy Consumption of E-COPS, AGDA, FBORP and OTP. It has been examined that the energy required by the proposed OTP algorithm is minimum compared to all other protocols E-COPS, AGDA, and FBORP.

Table 3.6 Energy Consumption of OTP, E-COPS, AGDA, and FBORP – Case 1

Simulation Time (ms)	Energy Consumption (J)			
	OTP	E-COPS	AGDA	AGDA
0	0	0	0	0
10	0.010233	0.013494	0.012407	0.011502
20	0.012123	0.016727	0.014259	0.014378
30	0.013114	0.021087	0.015992	0.017843
40	0.015438	0.031524	0.017724	0.021308
50	0.017523	0.027100	0.020457	0.024773
60	0.021070	0.032411	0.022989	0.027238
70	0.020612	0.035721	0.024922	0.030203
80	0.022355	0.038388	0.026154	0.033168
90	0.024213	0.043782	0.028087	0.035633
100	0.025831	0.044462	0.030919	0.039098

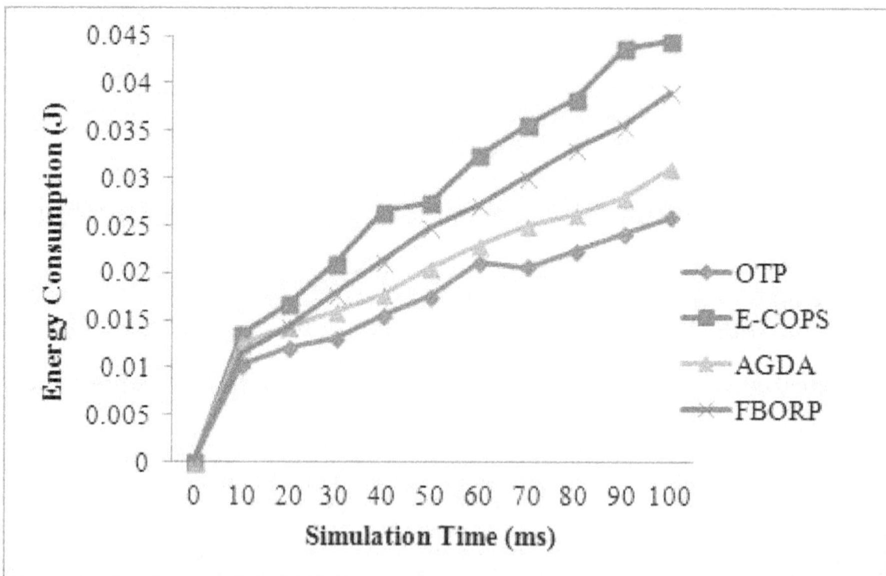

Figure 3.4 Energy Consumption of OTP, E-COPS, AGDA, and FBORP – Case 1

The proposed OTP has consumed 36.21%, 11.02% and 30.11% smaller energy than FBORP, E-COPS and AGDA protocols, respectively. As the proposed OTP algorithm discovers a suitable intermediate node based on its energy and relative angle, the energy preservation is minimal than the E-COPS algorithm as shown in Figure 3.4.

- **Delay**

A delay caused in MANETs is an important metric to be assessed during data or control packet reception and retransmission to verify the effectiveness of the protocol being implemented. The typical end-to-end delay during transmission in the underlying network is estimated by subtracting the amount of time required to receive all packets at the destination from the amount of time required for transmitting all the packets. Equation (3.6) is utilized to measure the delay value.

by using the equation (3.6).

$$\text{Delay} = \frac{1}{n}\left(\sum_{0}^{n} \text{PktTrans}_{\text{Time}}(n) - \text{pktR}_{\text{Time}}(n)\right) \tag{3.6}$$

Where 'n' represents the total number of packets being sent, $\text{PktTrans}_{\text{time}}$represents packet transmitted time and $\text{PktR}_{\text{time}}$ represents packet received time. Table 3.7 depicts the end-to-end delay caused during data transmission against different simulation time.

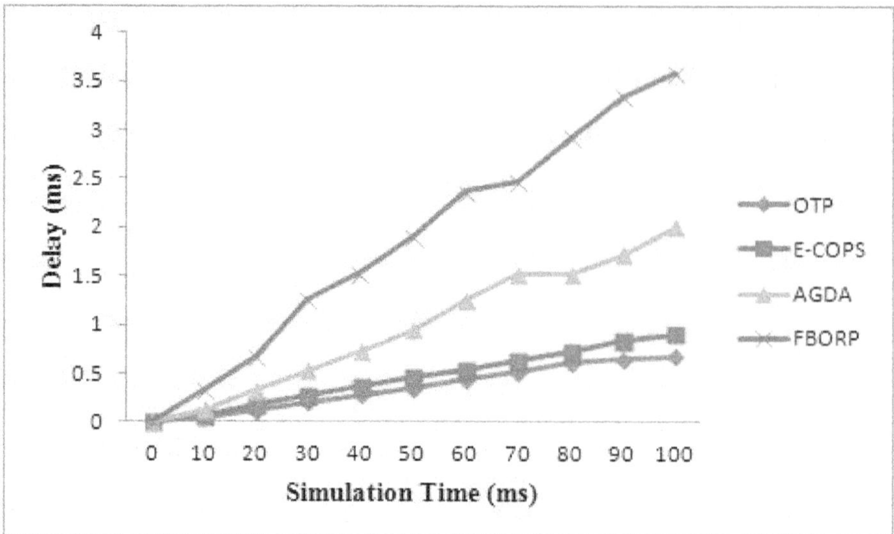

Figure 3.5 Delay of OTP, E-COPS, AGDA, and FBORP – Case 1

Table 3.7 Delay of OTP, E-COPS, AGDA and FBORP – Case 1

Simulation Time (ms)	Delay Time (ms)			
	OTP	E-COPS	AGDA	FBORP
0	0	0	0	0
10	0.0481	0.0643	0.124231	0.326125
20	0.1219	0.1784	0.324645	0.673975
30	0.2012	0.2642	0.524165	1.262685
40	0.2753	0.3641	0.725495	1.533155
50	0.3461	0.4544	0.937135	1.900175
60	0.4353	0.5354	1.247724	2.369972
70	0.5156	0.6301	1.517125	2.478975
80	0.6021	0.7245	1.517345	2.927072
90	0.6516	0.8364	1.719925	3.343758
100	0.6721	0.9014	1.99861	3.586775

Figure 3.5 shows that the delay in FBORP is higher when compared with OTP. This indicates that the delay time of the proposed OTP is less than all the existing solutions. In addition, the time needed to recover from failure links and retransmission is minimal thereby the performance of the proposed OTP has been optimized.

- **Packet LossRatio**

The packet loss ratio (PLR) represents the total number of packets lost during transmission per unit timethat is typically measured using total packet loss divided by sum of total packets received and total packets dropped. PLR is one of the very important metrics that indicates the entire network performance. PLR is calculated by using the Equation (3.7).

$$PLR = \frac{\sum_{0}^{n} pktL(n)}{\sum_{0}^{n} pktR(n) + \sum_{0}^{n} pktL(n)} \tag{3.7}$$

Table 3.8 PLR of OTP, E-COPS, AGDA and FBORP – Case 1

Simulation Time (ms)	PLR (%)			
	OTP	E-COPS	AGDA	FBROP
0	0	0	0	0
10	0.253	0.258	0.241	0.064
20	0.321	0.287	0.187	0.125
30	0.352	0.295	0.186	0.098
40	0.365	0.293	0.188	0.097
50	0.360	0.286	0.173	0.082
60	0.360	0.285	0.189	0.072
70	0.360	0.288	0.257	0.071
80	0.363	0.288	0.189	0.075
90	0.363	0.289	0.189	0.072
100	0.363	0.289	0.187	0.072

Table 3.8 depicts the simulated PLR values of different protocols including the proposed OTP. Figure 3.6 demonstrates the packet loss rate by the simulated network and it points out that the averaged PLR value of the proposed OTP is 10 %, 20 % and 33 % less than the existing E-COPS, AGDA and FBROP protocols, respectively.

The various simulation results point out that the OTP outperforms all other existing protocols.

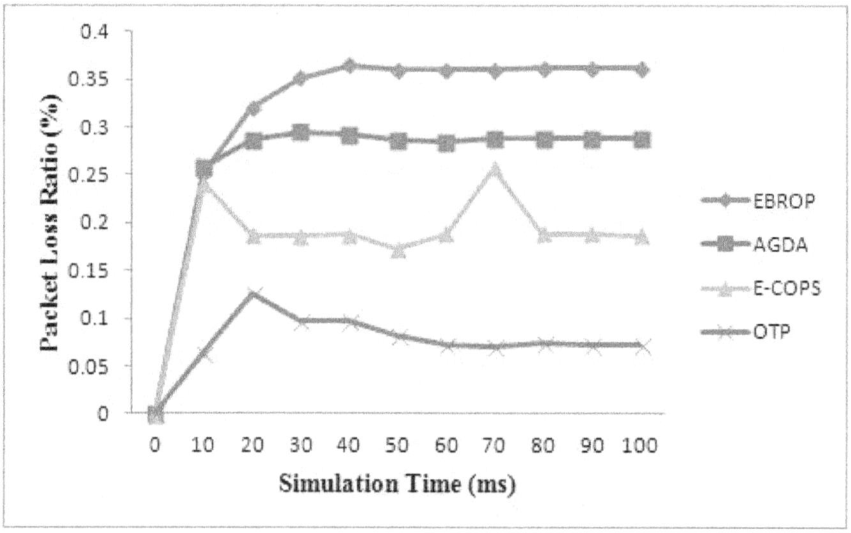

Figure 3.6 PLR of OTP, E-COPS, AGDA, and FBORP – Case 1

- **Throughput**

The total amount of data packets transmitted in a MANET using multiple intermediate hops is considered as the throughput of the underlying network. The overall performance of the MANET protocol being deployed depends on the amount of throughput achieved. Table 3.9 shows different values of the throughput attained by OTP, E-COPS, AGDA, and FBROP.

The throughput obtained for different protocols are depicted in Figure 3.7. By comparing the proposed OTP against the existing protocols,

Figure 3.7 shows that the proposed OTP has the throughputs of 43 %, 48 % and 58 %higher than E-COPS, AGDA and FBROP respectively. In short, the proposed OTP has improved the throughput rate to certain level under flat network topology.

Table 3.9 Throughput of OTP, E-COPS, AGDA, and FBROP – Case 1

Simulation Time (ms)	Throughput (bps)			
	OTP	E-COPS	AGDA	FBROP
0	0	0	0	0
10	235.289	334.382	283.462	187.704
20	989.134	699.588	591.544	510.770
30	1533.175	1043.273	966.676	734.687
40	2259.314	1423.105	1201.108	1016.464
50	2889.749	1755.747	1590.241	1305.841
60	3577.361	2174.282	1923.672	1568.329
70	4222.097	2475.629	2244.804	1832.304
80	4769.804	2826.388	2566.736	2107.687
90	5523.554	3112.118	2885.767	2368.965
100	6027.551	3526.759	3184.688	2617.989

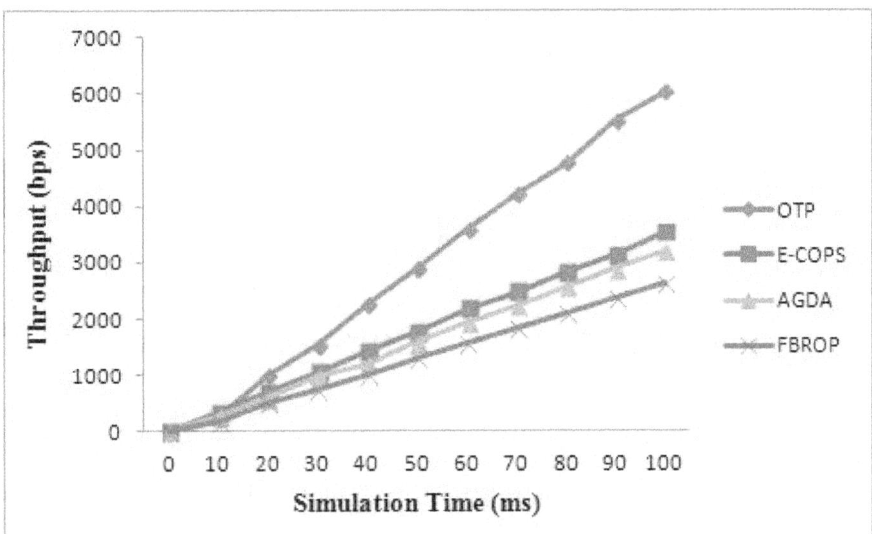

Figure 3.7 Throughput of OTP, E-COPS, AGDA, and FBORP – Case 1

3.3.2 Simulation Environment 2 – Hierarchical Network Topology

As case 2, the hierarchical network topology is setup for simulating the performance of the proposed OTP protocol to ensure its performance. Various metrics like PDR, Energy Consumption, Delay, PLR, and Throughput are calculated in case 2 as well.

- **Packet DeliveryRatio**

In order to measure the PDR in the hierarchical network topology, the same formula as given in equation (3.5) is utilized to estimate the packet delivery ratio against the OTP, E-COPS, and AGDA protocols. Different PDR values have been obtained during simulation which is specified in Table 3.10.

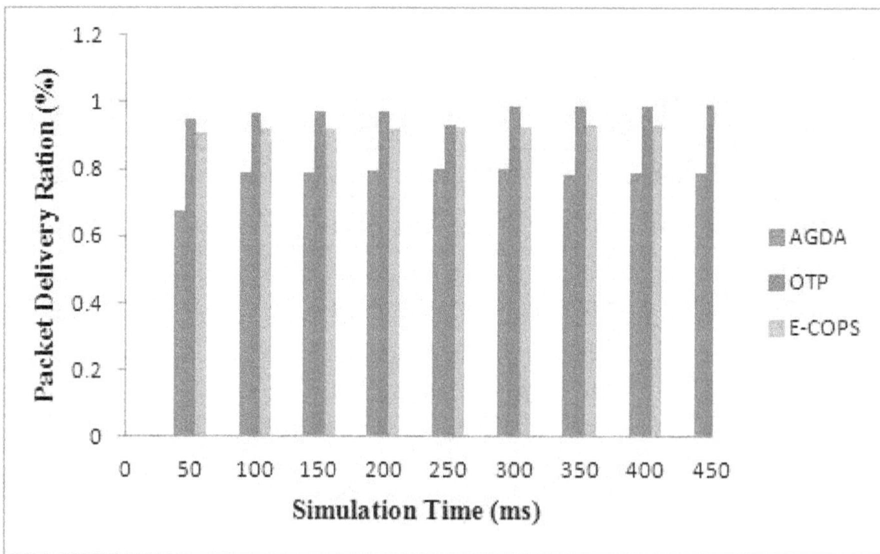

Figure 3.8 PDR of OTP, E-COPS and AGDA– Case 2

The values tabulated in Table 3.9 and the graph depicted in Figure 3.8 demonstrate the overall performance of the proposed OTP over E-COPS and AGDA protocols. The proposed OTP has achieved 19.9% better PDR than AGDA and 6 % better PDR than E-COPS protocols.

Table 3.10 PDR of AGDA, E-COPS and OTP – Case 2

Simulation Time (ms)	PDR		
	AGDA	OTP	E-COPS
0	1	1	1
50	0.678	0.949	0.911
100	0.787	0.967	0.918
150	0.791	0.969	0.919
200	0.796	0.974	0.919
250	0.798	0.929	0.925
300	0.799	0.986	0.928
350	0.784	0.989	0.929
400	0.787	0.988	0.931
450	0.789	0.993	0.939

- **Energy Consumption**

The residual energy of the nodes,i.e.,Energy Consumption metric for the OTP, E-COPS and AGDA are determined and final results obtained aregiven in Table 3.11.

Table 3.11Energy Consumption of AGDA, E-COPS and OTP – Case 2

Simulation Time (ms)	Energy Consumption (J)		
	AGDA	OTP	E-COPS
0	0.020475	0.010254	0.0206
50	0.058134	0.045632	0.0509
100	0.09895	0.067231	0.0774
150	0.124709	0.075763	0.0977
200	0.154723	0.115616	0.1307s
250	0.166578	0.136754	0.1568
300	0.19999	0.140552	0.1838
350	0.240576	0.162510	0.1998
400	0.275489	0.196446	0.2359
450	0.299788	0.219377	0.2787

Table 3.10 shows the values of the AGDA, OTP and E-COPS protocols obtained during simulation analysis. Figure 3.9 indicates that the performance efficiency in terms of energy consumption of the proposed OTP in hierarchical network topology requires only minimal. OTP requires 23 % lesser amount of energy than AGDA and 14 % reduced amount of energy than E-COPS protocols. Therefore, OTP outperforms all other protocols.

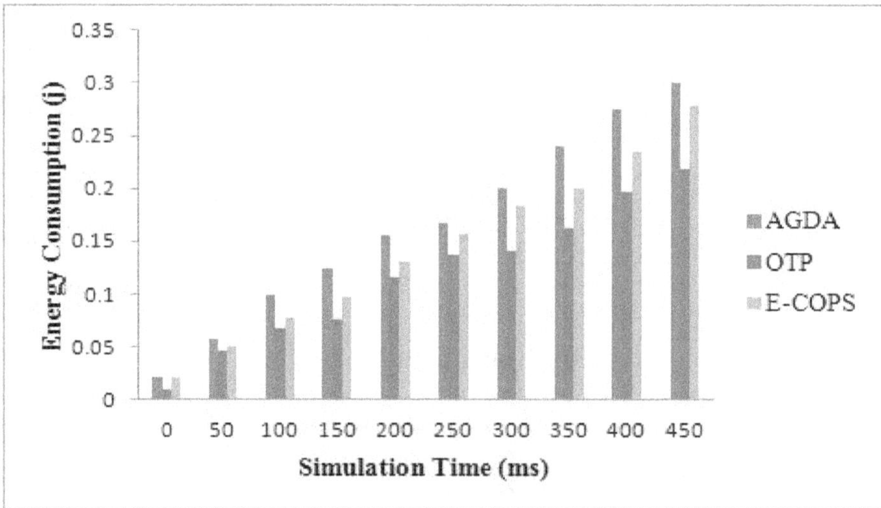

Figure 3.9 Energy Consumption of AGDA, E-COPS and OTP – Case 2

- **Delay**

The delay times between a source node and its communicating node with a network is measured using the equation 3.6 for FBROP, AGDA, and OTP protocols. The simulated delay time of the existing protocols including the proposed OTP has been obtained and given in Table 3.12 and plotted as shown in the Figure 3.10.

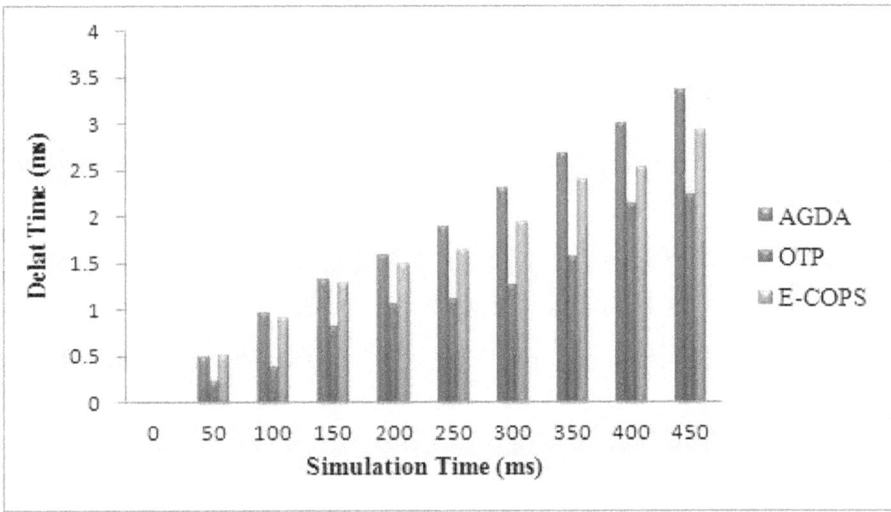

Figure 3.10 Delay time of AGDA, E-COPS and OTP – Case 2

It has been observed that the delay time of proposed OTP is less when compared with AGDA and E-COPS protocol.

Table 3.12 Delay time of AGDA, E-COPS and OTP – Case 2

Simulation Time (ms)	Delay time (ms)		
	AGDA	OTP	E-COPS
0	0	0	0
50	0.479677	0.2101	0.4927
100	0.952862	0.3674	0.8955
150	1.312843	0.8103	1.2667
200	1.578839	1.04401	1.4837
250	1.887565	1.1130	1.6279
300	2.297658	1.2521	1.9299
350	2.674116	1.5564	2.3943
400	2.996543	2.1329	2.5268
450	3.357866	2.2163	2.9284

- **Packet LossRatio**

The PLR value caused in the underlying network is also obtained and verified using equation 3.7 for AGDA, E-COPS, and OTP protocols as simulation environment.

Table 3.13 depicts the PLR values computed against AGDA, AGDA and OTP mechanisms. Figure 3.12 demonstrates the plots inferred from the values tabulated in Table 3.13.

From Figure 3.11, it is inferred that the PLR value of AGDA is 27% larger than OTP and the PLR value of E-COPS is 15 % larger than AGDA protocols. It is inferred that the smaller value of PLR indicates the corresponding increase in the PLR value of the proposed OTP.

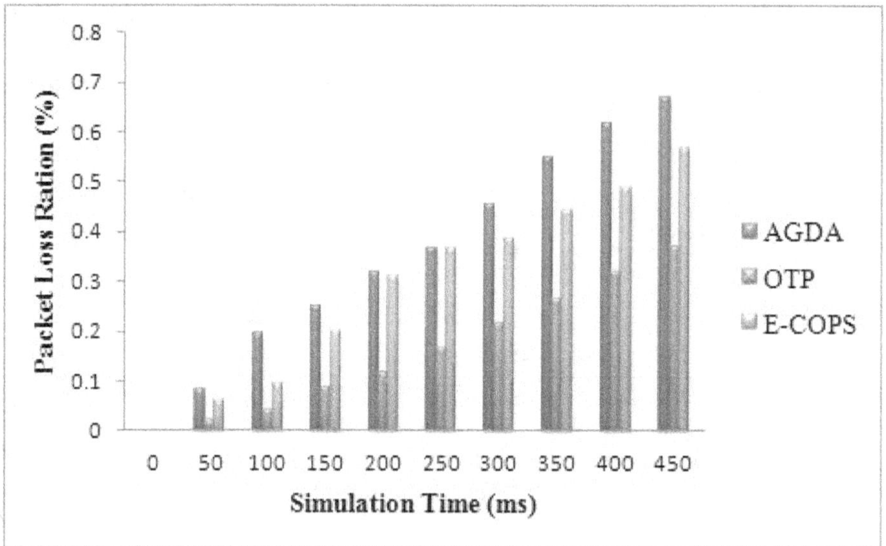

Figure 3.11 PLR of ADGA, E-COPS and OTP – Case 2

Table 3.13 PLR of ADGA, E-COPS and OTP – Case 2

Simulation Time (ms)	PLR (%)		
	AGDA	OTP	E-COPS
0	0	0	0
50	0.0809	0.0211	0.0591
100	0.1963	0.0423	0.0954
150	0.2498	0.0880	0.1986
200	0.31811	0.1175	0.3106
250	0.3674	0.1643	0.3672
300	0.4537	0.2163	0.3844
350	0.5486	0.2652	0.4415
400	0.6187	0.3174	0.4868
450	0.6709	0.3721	0.5666

- **Throughput**

The throughput also indicates the performance of the underlying MANETs. The simulation environment is setup with 50 nodes to measure the throughput of AGDA, E-COPS, and OTP and put into the Table 3.14.

Table 3.14 Throughput of AGDA, E-COPS and OTP – Case 2

Simulation Time (ms)	Throughput (bps)		
	AGDA	OTP	E-COPS
0	0	0	0
50	450670	999845	739657
100	550532	1423462	1035201
150	651571	1667347	1157343
200	747826	1878984	1267390
250	832865	2109374	1378257
300	912345	2356920	1436766
350	989234	2525784	1425447
400	1034770	2689290	1544680
450	1045805	2859047	1521465

The throughput of the different protocolstaken into consideration has been obtained and these values are plotted as shown in Figure3.12.

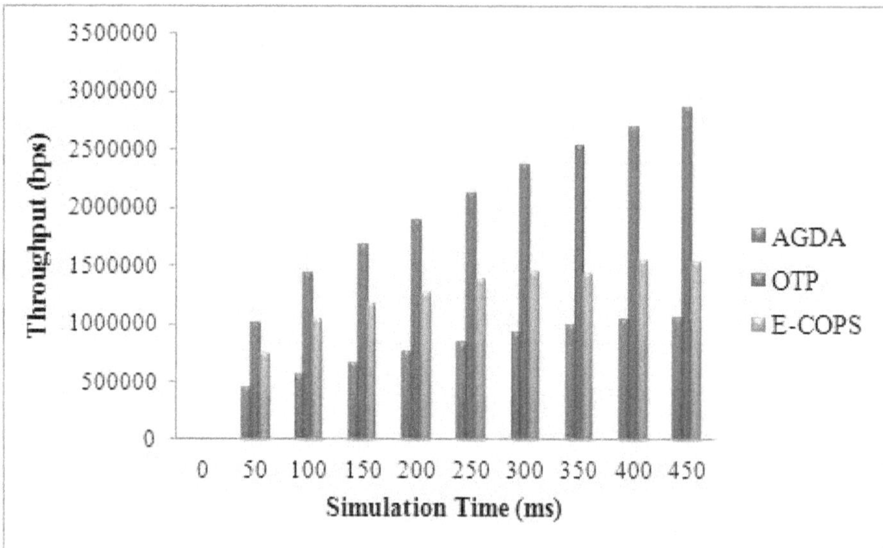

Figure 3.12 Throughput of AGDA, E-COPS and OTP – Case 2

It has been observed from the Figure 3.12 that the throughput value of OTP is estimated to be 59 % better than AGDA protocol. OTP has improved throughput, i.e., 39 % than the AGDA protocol. The improved throughput of OTP has also proved its efficiency.

3.4 SUMMARY

In this Chapter, a novel OTP algorithm for establishing energy efficient optimal path in a MANET has been proposed, implemented and evaluated. If a CM node wants to transmit data packet to its communicating node should forward it to the CH node which is responsible to forward the packet to the base station. If both the base station and CH node are not in the same transmission range, then the CH node might choose multiple intermediate hops. The proposed OTP algorithm discovers an optimal path based on the relative angle and energy availability of each next hop.

The OTP offers a better performance in MANETs when comparing against existing protocols like AGDA, E-COPS and FBROP both in the flat and hierarchical network environments. A separate assessment of the proposed OTP in the hierarchical network environment of MANETs is executed against AGDA and E-COPS. The simulation analysis has confirmed that the proposed multi-hop protocol achieves lesser PLR, lower Energy Consumption, improved throughput and PDR than existing protocols. Thus the lifetime of the current network is increased through discovering optimal energy efficient shortest path.

CHAPTER 4

DISCOVERY OF OPTIMAL MULTICAST ROUTES IN MANETS USING CROSS-LAYER APPROACH AND FUZZY LOGIC SUPPORT SYSTEM

Due to the dynamic behaviour and nature of the network topology of MANETs, providing a reliable and highly stable route for transmitting either data or control packet to a collaborative working group becomes challenging. This chapter presents a fuzzy decision system based Cross layer optimized Multicast Routing Protocol (C-MRP), which addresses and overcomes the issue of Ad Hoc multicast on-demand table routing protocol. We integrate a light weight fuzzy set of rules to select optimal multicast routes to destination nodes using parameters such as route stability, available bandwidth and delay.

A comparative analysis of all the simulated results are analyzed using two proposed mechanisms including the existing solutions and protocols that are presented and discussed in this chapter. The performance of the underlying Ad Hoc network topology is determined and analyzed from discovering an optimal route among the proposed protocol against existing solutions and protocols.

4.1 PREAMBLE

The Open System Interconnect model is composed of seven layers namely, physical layer, data link layer, network layer, transport layer, session layer, presentation layer and application layer. The layers involved when information is transferred from one machine to another machine it may travel through many intermediate notes. These intermediate nodes usually involve only the first three layers of the OSI reference model.

Traditional layered protocol stack model used in all new communication systems is not suitable for MANETs. The traditional architecture splits the entire function of overall network into seven layers and each layer has separate predefined services in hierarchical order and blocks direct communication between nonadjacent layers. It faces more challenges to improve service quality of underlying network with improved data delivery to the receivers. The cross layer design framework optimizes the function of a node by breaking the entire structure of layered model as depicted in Figure 4.1.

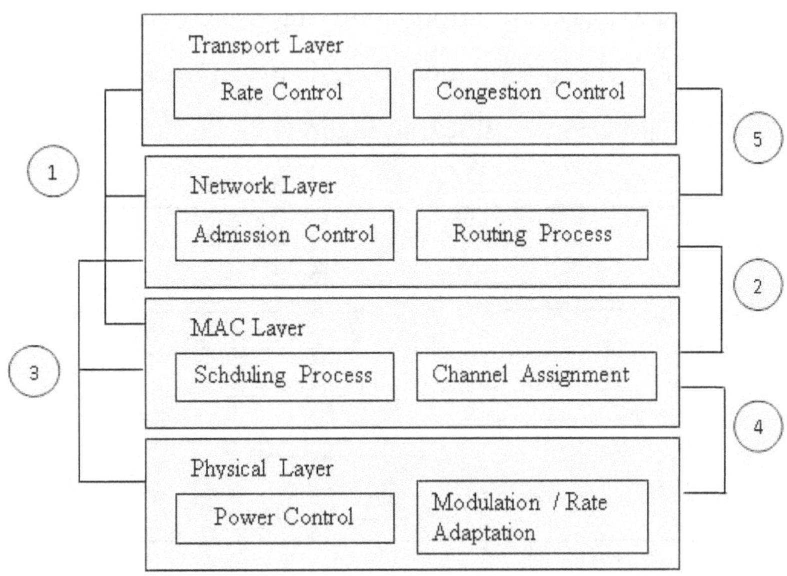

Figure 4.1 Cross Layer based Protocol Architecture

The cross-layer interaction design permits interaction among multiple layers for improving system performance and information exchange takes place among lower layers, network layer and transport layer. The parameters associated with modes are controlled in distinct layers in Ad Hoc network. In cross layer interaction design framework, the parameters of the link layer and physical layer are mainly used to diminish the noise ratio and interference level. In addition, the network layer is responsible for optimal route selection. The cross layer interaction design approach improves the relationship among different layers (Setton*et al.* 2005,

Winter *et al.* 2006), and (Zhang and Zhang, 2008) also improves the QoS to certain extent.

4.2 FUZZY LOGIC BASED MANETs

Fuzzy Inference Process (FIP) is the way of devising input/output (I/O) maps from fuzzy logic rules and the inputs/outputs to FIP are crisp in nature. And, both fuzzification process and defuzzification process are required to translate crisp information into fuzzy representation (Nicola andZorzi, 2008). The information flow between various components in a fuzzy inference process is outlined in Figure 4.2.

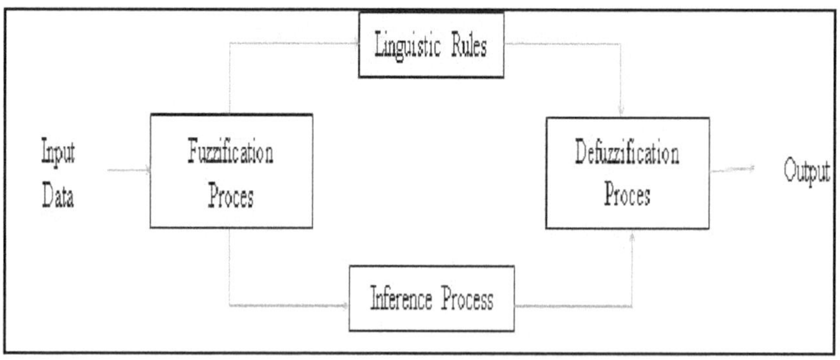

Figure 4.2 Fuzzy Inference Process

4.3 FUZZIFIER

The fuzzifier module gets more than two crisp parameters as inputs and renovates them into fuzzy membership function values, which lie between 0 to 1. The function may be triangle or trapezoid that depends on the available points that define a member function. The fuzzy decision building process includes a fuzzy set in the type of IF-THEN rules. The fuzzy output is established from the rules framed in the system. The rules to be applied can change and depend on the membership functions which are used to decide the outcome.

4.4 DE-FUZZIFIER

The final outcome from fuzzy is then applied to transform into a crisp data. For defuzzification process, various mathematical approaches are used, such as center of gravity method.

4.5 KNOWLEDGE BASED FUZZY SYSTEM

It defines the link between crisp input/output parameters and their fuzzy representation, which is understood by the fuzzy controller. From practical implementation, the description of each input/output variable is listed as below:

- The domain over which the variable can assume values.
- A defined linguistic type of attributes ("labels") that compose its qualitative representation.
- Membership functions for each label.

4.6 PROPOSED C-MRP ALGORITHM

An optimal multicast route discovery in MANETs using cross-layer and fuzzy rules is proposed and demonstrated. The proposed C-MRP mechanism uses an OTP algorithm to discover energy efficient intermediate nodes and improves the life-time of the Ad Hoc network to certain extent.

From the existing solutions and literature survey, we extracted the information to discover an optimized route to a group of communicating mobile nodes. By altering a few important parameters in the existing multicast route discovery protocols, the efficacy of the C-MRP routing algorithm is enhanced. The algorithm for discovering optimal path between nodes is illustrated in Table 4.1.

Table 4.1 Pseudo code to detect the first power energized intermediate node

Line	**Procedure:** Optimal Path Selection
1	**begin**
2	**if** (source node) transmits message (group of destination nodes) **then**
3	{ check the availability of route;
4	**if** (available) then goto Step 19; }
5	**else**
6	(source node) broadcasts (route request message) through intermediate nodes;
7	**endif**
8	**if** (intermediary node) maintains a route (to the destination) **then** start transmission;
9	**else** rebroadcasts the route request message to all its neighbors;
10	**endif**
11	intermediate nodes ← establish reverse route;
12	(node that receives RREQ) ← reply and stores its sequence number;
13	(node that receives RREP) ← updates the source-destination address, previous hop, existing
14	battery power, quality of the current route and current network bandwidth;
15	(source node) ← computes (route stability and current network bandwidth from RREP);
16	(values computed by source in step 6) ← inputs to the fuzzy logic system);
17	(source node) ← select a best route with high route stability-bandwidth;
18	(source node) transmit a data to destination.
19	**End**

Fuzzy logic system – It involves fuzzify the current input values of residual bandwidth and route stability. The residual bandwidth and route stability are extracted from these parameters and such inputs are assigned a degree with suitable fuzzy sets. Actually, the input values are crisp which are derived from PS and BWres.

We consider three possibilities such as low, medium, and high for representing stability and bandwidth values. The bandwidth (residual) and stability of a path are provided as inputs and its output represents the Optimized Path, which is referred as OP for transmitting data. Table 4.2 demonstrates different combinations of stability and bandwidth using fuzzy logic.

Fuzzy system for making decisions - The combination of availability of network bandwidth and route stability define the following rules that are used in fuzzy logic supporting system and give the optimal route. The rules for inferring a decision from the fuzzy logic supporting system are listed from rule [0] to rule [8] as tabulated in Table 4.3.

Table 4.2 System of stability and bandwidth values

		Bandwidth		
		Low	Medium	High
Stability	Low	LB, LS	LB,MS	LB,HS
	Medium	MB,LS	MB,MS	MB,HS
	High	HB,LS	HB,MS	HB,HS

Table 4.3 Fuzzy logic rules

Rule	Comment
rules[0]	low Stability and low network Bandwidth, then optimal path exhibits very low
rules[1]	medium Stability and low Bandwidth, then optimal path exhibits low
rules[2]	low Bandwidth and high Stability, then optimal path exhibits low
rules[3]	medium Bandwidth and low Stability then optimal path exhibits medium
rules[4]	medium Bandwidth and medium Stability then optimal path exhibits medium
rules[5]	medium Bandwidth and high Stability then optimal path exhibits high
rules[6]	low Stability with high Bandwidth, then optimal path exhibits low
rules[7]	high Bandwidth and medium Stability then optimal path exhibits high
rules[8]	high Bandwidth and high Stability then optimal path exhibits very high

Figure 4.3, Figure 4.4 and Figure 4.5 depict the relationship among bandwidth input, path stability and optimal path, which utilizes the triangle function.

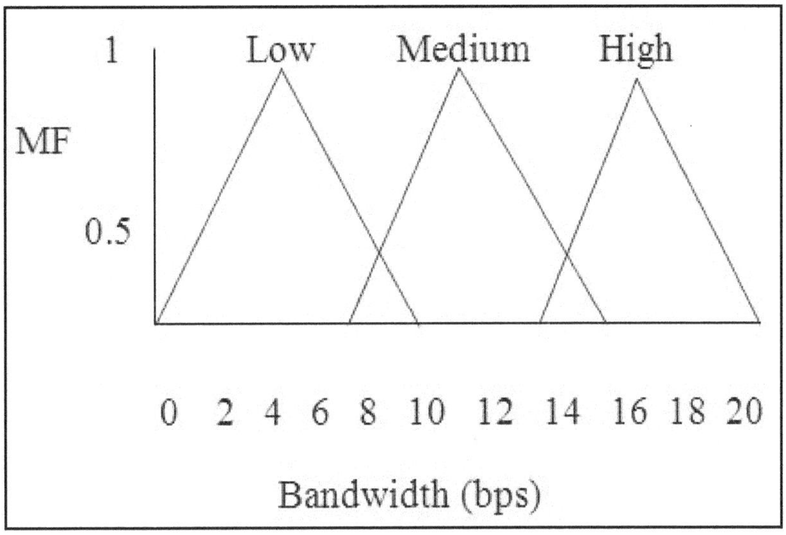

Figure 4.3 Membership function Vs bandwidth input

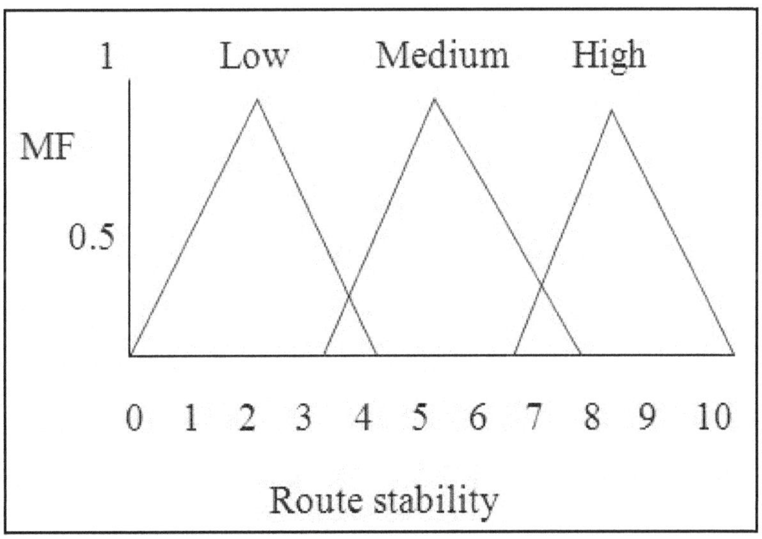

Figure 4.4 Membership function Vs path stability

Defuzzification - The technique by which a crispy value is inferred from fuzzy logic set for representing an exact value is recognized as defuzzification. In order to calculate the area of centroid area, we apply defuzzification process. The formula (4.1) illustrates the calculation of defuzzification process.

$$Fuzzy - cost = \frac{all\ rules\ z_i \times \lambda(z_i)}{all\ rules\ \lambda(z_i)} \quad (4.1)$$

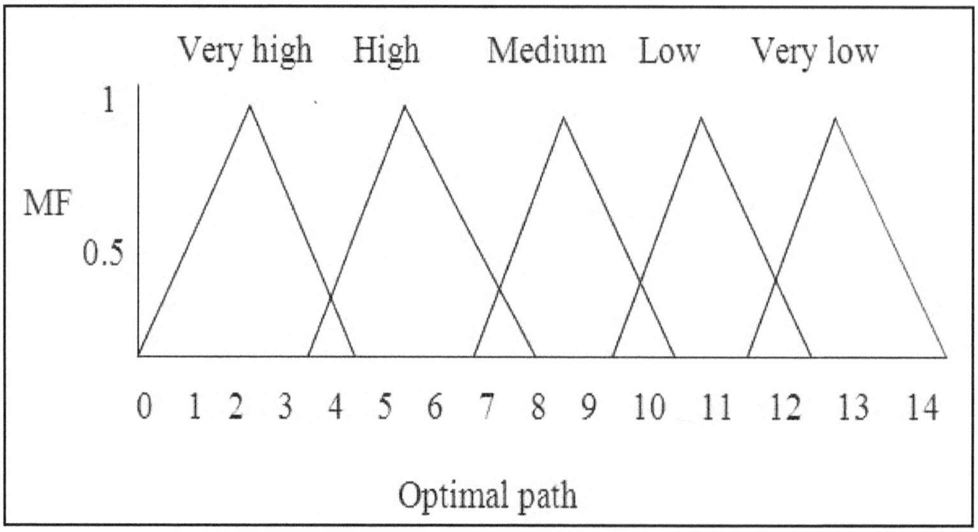

Figure 4.5 Membership function Vs optimal path

The fuzzy-cost is mainly utilized to state the grade of decision making, z_i denotes the fuzzy all rules and its corresponding membership function. The outcome of the fuzzy-cost function is crisp value in nature which can be produced from defuzzification process (Fotis*et al.* 2008). Thus, the chosen optimal path is mainly utilized for transmitting actual data from any source node to any destination node.

As depicted in Table 3.2, to select an optimal energy efficient path/route, the source mobile node checks the energy of the first intermediate mobile node. If the energy of that node is high (greater than 90 percent), the source node extends its coverage distance with next node by applying the same procedure. When the energy is lower than the predefined value, then the source node determines its relative angle to discover an energy efficient intermediate node. This process is repeated until a stable and optimal path is discovered.

4.7 EXPERIMENTATION AND DISCUSSION

In this section, we outline the simulation environment, results and discussion about the proposed C-MRP protocol which is implemented in NS2 with radio transmission range of $(100\times 100)\ m^2$.

The destination location is located 100 m away with channel capacity of 2 Mbps. We consider UDP protocol, source and sink with CBR traffic for simulation.

4.7.1 Parameters Exercised

In this section we explain some important parameters that are used to show the efficacy of the proposed C-MRP protocol.

4.7.1.1 Bandwidth estimation

Any node that wants to communicate to the group of destination mobile nodes calculates its local bandwidth and neighbour's bandwidth information within the sensing range. This is because of reasons such as sharing bandwidth between Neighbouring nodes, paying attention to different channels and estimating local bandwidth. It mostly relies on the channel idle time period and its busy time period, which is fixed as a predefined time interval (Mohammed *et al.* 2006). The accessible bandwidth between two adjacent mobile nodes is calculated as follows.

$$Bandwidth(Loc) = C \times (T_i / T_t) \qquad (4.2)$$

Where, C denotes the channel's capacity,

T_i denotes the channel's idle time period and

T_t represents the channel's active time period

$$Bandwidth(res) = Bandwidth(Loc) - Bandwidth(Min) \tag{4.3}$$

Where, Bandwidth (res) = Residual Bandwidth

Bandwidth (Loc) = Local Bandwidth

Bandwidth (Min) = Minimum Bandwidth

4.7.1.2 Estimation of route stability

This process involves measuring the accessible battery power, distance, and route quality values retrieved dynamically from MAC and PHY layers. Route stability is decided from the aforementioned parameters (Prasad *et al.* 2011) using equation (4.4).

$$Route\ Stability = \left(\frac{P_{ij} \times RQ_{ij}}{D_{ij}} \right) \tag{4.4}$$

Node battery Power (P_{ij})

It is computed as ratio between power obtained at source mobile node and power transferred by *neighbour* node and is measured as follows.

$$P_{ij} = \frac{P_{rx}}{P_{tx}} \tag{4.5}$$

Where, P_{rx} represents the power obtained at the source mobile node and

P_{tx}denotes power transmitted by a Neighbouring mobile node.

Route quality (RQ_{ij})

It is measured from the value of Expected data Transmission Time (E_{tt}). The E_{tt} value for a specific route is predicted from the value of anticipated transmission time by exchanging a single data packet with MAC layer. The E_{tt} time can be attained by summing all values of E_{tt} of the distinct links of the route.

$$E_{tt} = E_{tx} \times \left(\frac{K}{BW_{link}}\right) \tag{4.6}$$

Where, *k* represents the average data packet size, BW_{link} represents the current available link bandwidth and E_{tx} denotes the estimated transmission calculation.

The expected data transmission calculation (E_{tx}) is calculated by measuring link quality and route quality. The value of E_{tx} for a specific route is defined using equation (4.6).

$$E_{tx} = \frac{1}{(Pac_{tx} \times Pac_{rx})} \tag{4.7}$$

where, Pac_{tx}denotes the probability of successfully delivered packets in the forward direction and Pac_{rx} denotes the successful acknowledgment packet reception probability.

Distance (D_{ij})

It represents the distance between two nodes, which is computed by applying free space propagation model.

4.7.1.3 Estimation of delay between nodes

The delay between nodes covers propagation and transmission time delay, buffering delay while carrying out route discovery, queuing delay and resend delay. It is represented as the total time taken for actual data transmission by a source-destination pair (DimitriosandAli 2011).

$$D_{end} = \left(Td_{rx} - Td_{tx}\right) \tag{4.8}$$

Where, D_{end} denotes the end delay, Td_{rx} represents the data reception time and Td_{tx} denotes data transmission time.

4.7.1.4 Estimation of lost packet ratio (LPR)

Lost Packet Ratio (LPR) represents the overall number of data packets dropped during data transmission to a specific destination and is measured in terms of dropped data packets. Table 4.4 lists different simulation parameters that are exercised for evaluating the efficacy of the proposed C-MRP.

Table 4.4 Simulation Parameters

Nodes	50,75,100,125,150
Area Size	100× 100 m^2
MAC	802.11
Simulation Time	50 sec
Traffic Source	CBR
Packet Size	512 bytes
Rate	100kb
Transmission Range	150m
Speed of events	5 m/s
Pause time	5,10,15,20 and 25 sec

Flows	2,4,6 and 8

The efficacy of the proposed C-MRP protocol is compared with MAODV protocol (Meng*et al.* 2005), ODMRP protocol (Gerla*et al.* 2003) and PDTMRP protocol (Wang 2012). When we vary the communicating receivers as 10, 20, 30, 40 and 50 as shown in Table 4.5, the time delay variation has increased rapidly in MAODV protocol, ODMRP protocol and PDTMRP protocol and slowly increased in CBRM as revealed in Figure 4.6.

Table 4.5 Delay Time of MAODV, ODMRP, PDTMRP and C-MRP

No. of Receivers	Delay Time (Seconds)			
	MAODV	ODMRP	PDTMRP	C-MRP
10	0	0	0	0
20	15	13	17	10
30	25	21	24	17
40	34	30	36	22
50	42	38	40	28

The value of packer delivery ratio is high when the currently available receiver nodes are high, whereas delivery ratio may decrease when the currently communicating number of mobile nodes decreases, but C-MRP produces better result which is confirmed using Figure 4.7 and the simulated PDR values against different protocols are tabulated in Table 4.6.

When the currently communicating mobile nodes are increased, packet dropping can also increase but suddenly decrease to low level in all protocols, whereas packet drop increases when nodes are increased. However, packet drop in C-MRP is minimum as confirmed using Figure 4.8 and Table 4.7.

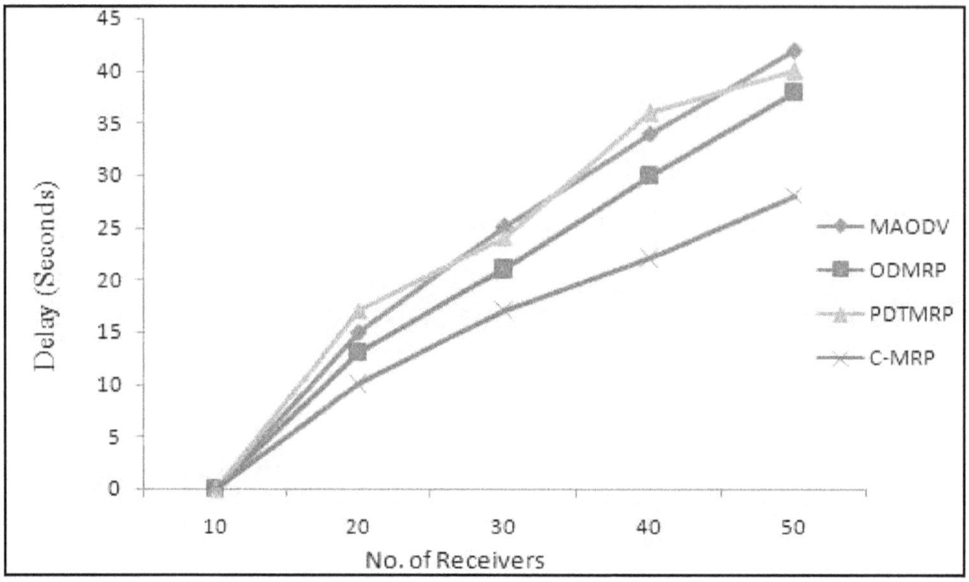

Figure 4.6 Receivers Vs Delay

Table 4.6 PDR of MAODV, ODMRP, PDTMRP and C-MRP

No. of Receivers	Packet Delivery Ratio (%)			
	MAODV	ODMRP	PDTMRP	C-MRP
10	4	3	5	2.8
20	4.2	3.5	4	3
30	3.6	3	3.5	2.6
40	2.9	2	2	2.2
50	1	1	1	1

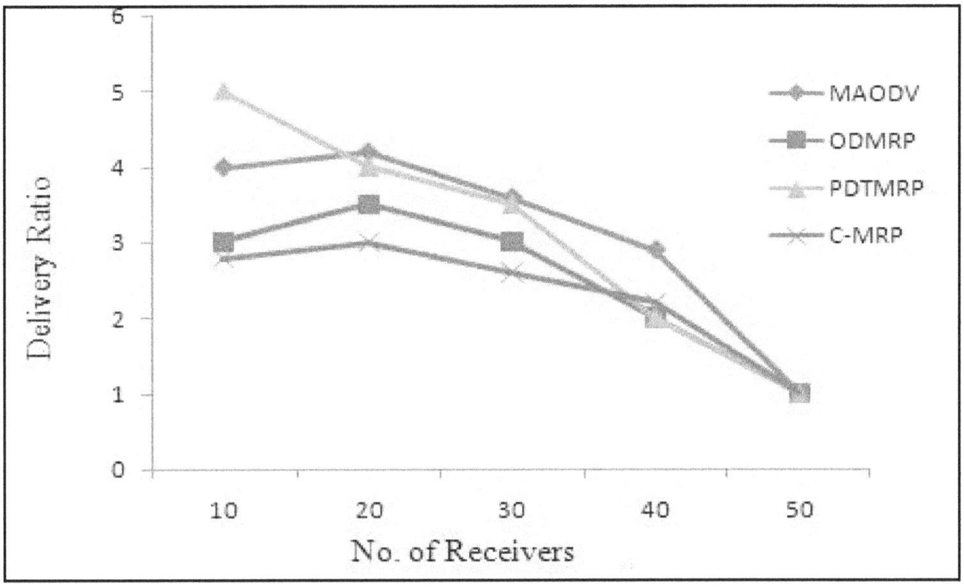

Figure 4.7 PDR Vs Receivers

The delay is increased slowly as the number of currently available mobile nodes increase but decrease at 125 nodes.

Table 4.7 Packet Drop of MAODV, ODMRP, PDTMRP and C-MRP

No. of Mobile Nodes	No. of Dropped Packets			
	MAODV	ODMRP	PDTMRP	C-MRP
50	14500	13000	14000	11000
75	16525	15000	16000	13000
100	16530	15000	16000	12900
125	13000	11500	12000	10500
150	17750	17000	17500	15000

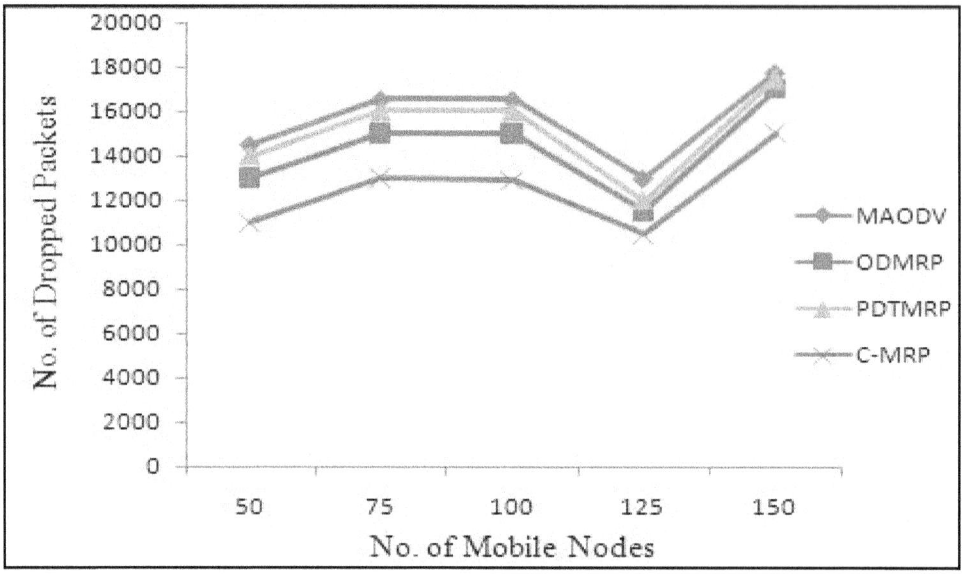

Figure 4.8 Nodes Vs Packet Drop

The proposed C-MRP protocol causes minimum delay than other solutions as confirmed from Figure 4.9 and Table 4.8. In addition, Figure 4.10 and Table 4.9 indicate that PDR values are continuously decreased when the currently communicating mobile nodes increase. But the PDR is also decreased when the total number of mobile nodes has increased to 125. However, the proposed C-MRP produces higher PDR than other protocols.

In this simulation scenario, pause time has been changed from 10 to 50 to calculate packet loss, delay and PDR without changing mobile nodes. Packet dropping is increased when pause time is gradually increased from 10 to 30.

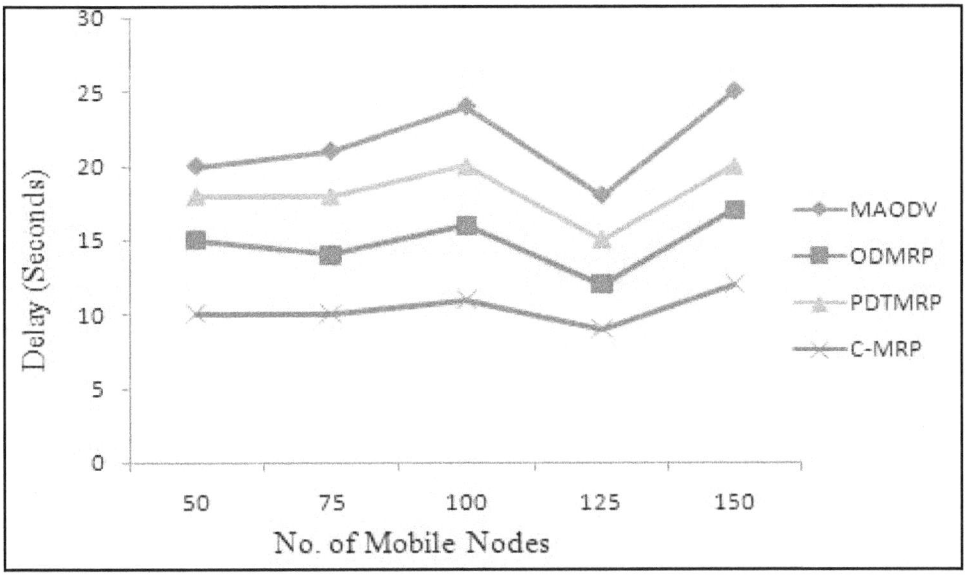

Figure 4.9 Nodes Vs Delay

Table 4.8 Delay Vs No. of nodes

No. of Nodes	Delay Time (Seconds)			
	MAODV	ODMRP	PDTMRP	C-MRP
50	20	15	18	10
75	21	14	18	10
100	24	16	20	11
125	18	12	15	9
150	25	17	20	12

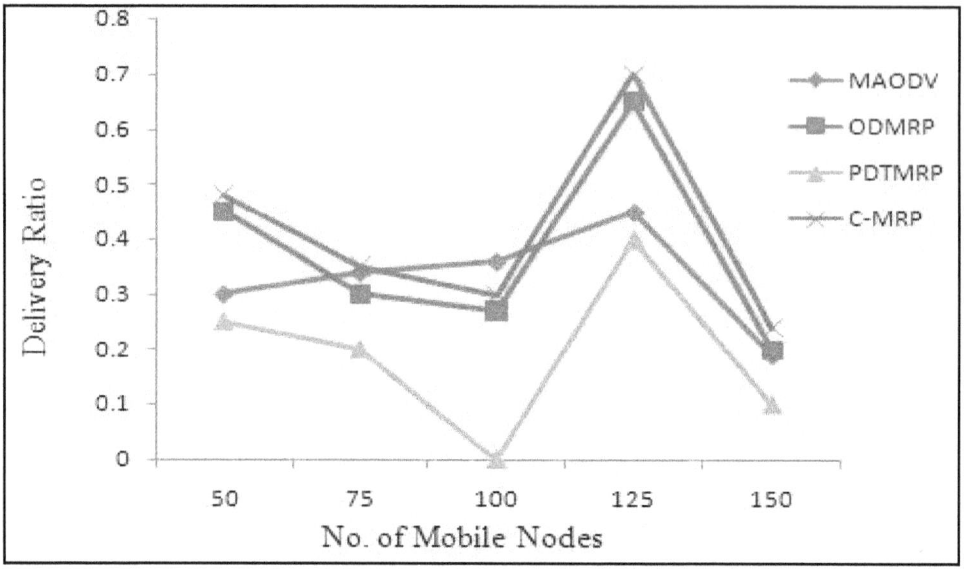

Figure 4.10 Mobile Nodes Vs PDR

Table 4.9 Delivery Ratio Vs No. of nodes

No. of nodes	Packet Delivery Ratio (%)			
	MAODV	ODMRP	PDTMRP	C-MRP
50	0.3	0.45	0.25	0.48
75	0.34	0.3	0.2	0.35
100	0.36	0.27	0	0.3
125	0.45	0.65	0.4	0.7
150	0.19	0.2	0.1	0.24

When the pause time is changed from 10 to 40 second, packet drop goes high and then it gets reduced. It shows that the number of packets dropped in the proposed C-MRP algorithm is less when compared with other algorithms as illustrated in Figure 4.11 and Table 4.10.

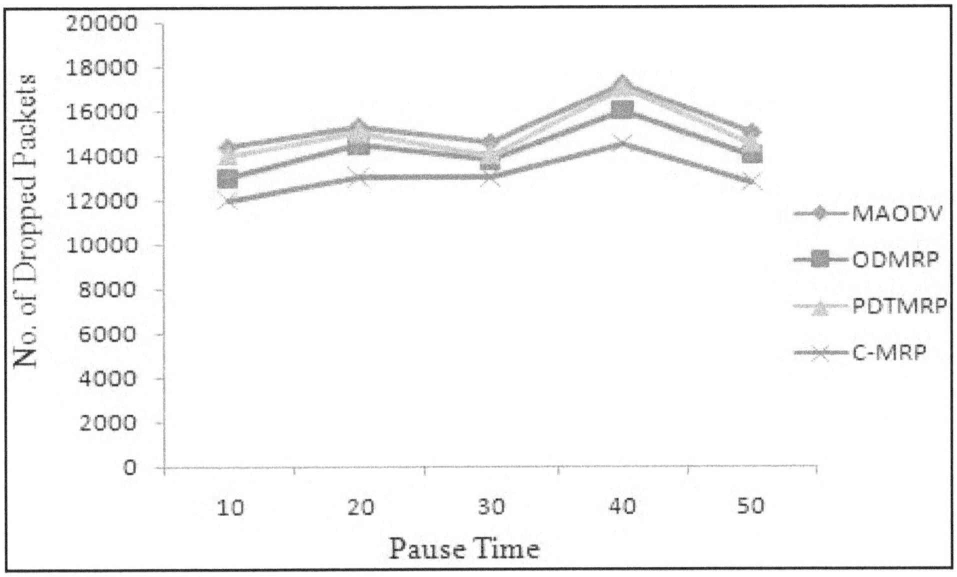

Figure 4.11 Pause Time Vs Packet Drop

Table 4.10 Pause Time Vs PDR

Pause Time (Seconds)	No. of Dropped Packets			
	MAODV	ODMRP	PDTMRP	C-MRP
10	14400	13000	14000	12000
20	15300	14500	15000	13000
30	14600	13750	14000	13000
40	17200	16000	17000	14500
50	15000	14000	14500	12790

The transmission delay time is low in our C-MRP protocol than existing protocols when we change pause time as confirmed from Figure 4.12 and the values tabulated in Table 4.11. The value of PDR also improves in C-MRP than existing protocols as indicated in Figure 4.13 and Table 4.12.

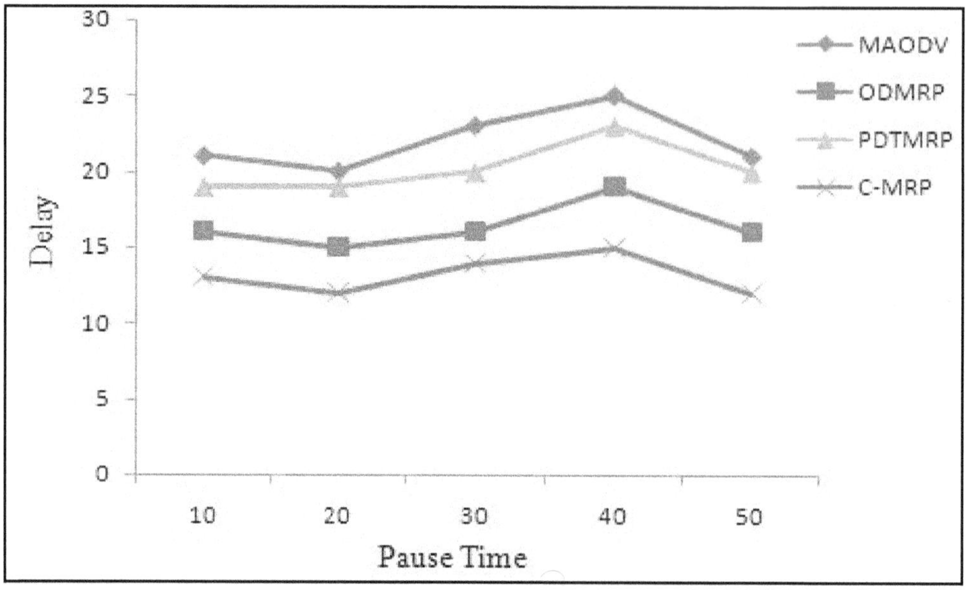

Figure 4.12 Mobile nodes Vs Delay

Table 4.11 Pause Time Vs Delay

Pause Time (Seconds)	Delay Time (ms)			
	MAODV	ODMRP	PDTMRP	C-MRP
10	21	16	19	13
20	20	15	19	12
30	23	16	20	14
40	25	19	23	15
50	21	16	20	12

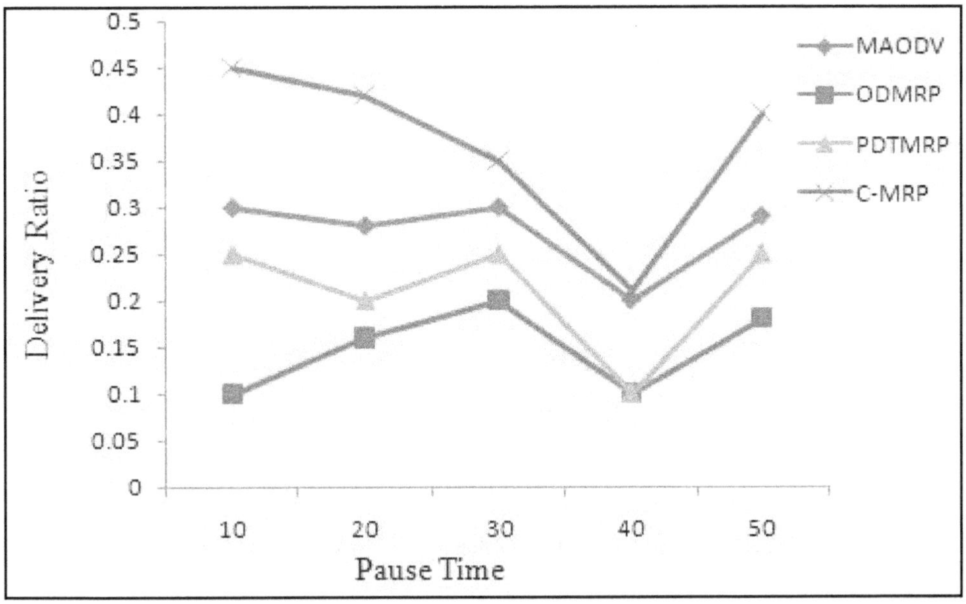

Figure 4.13 Pause time Vs Delivery ratio

Table 4.12 Pause Time Vs PLR

Pause Time (ms)	PDR (%)			
	MAODV	ODMRP	PDTMRP	C-MRP
10	0.3	0.1	0.25	0.45
20	0.28	0.16	0.2	0.42
30	0.3	0.2	0.25	0.35
40	0.2	0.1	0.1	0.21
50	0.29	0.18	0.25	0.4

The energy required for both transmitting and reception of either data packets or control packets in a MNAET will decide the life time of the current network topology. And it is calculated by using the initial available energy in a node and its average residual energy. The energy acquired by the three existing protocols and solutions is evaluated using simulation investigation.

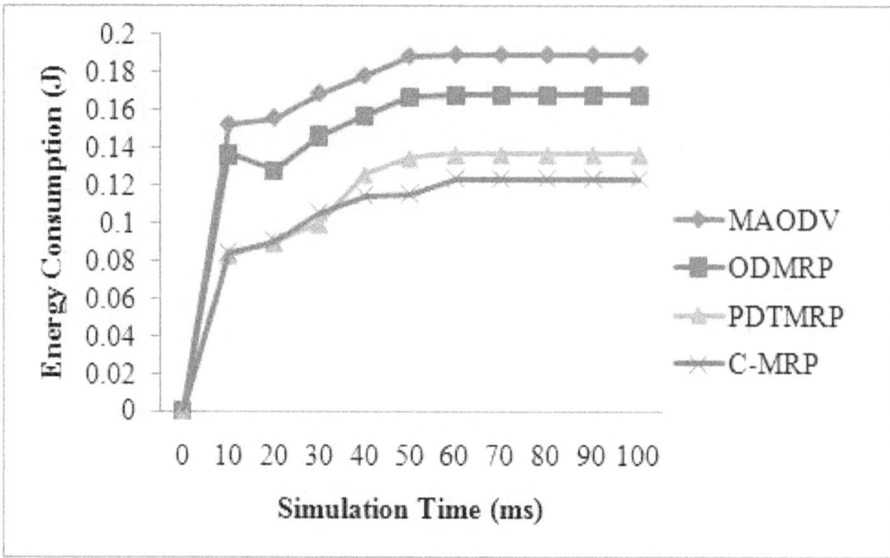

Figure 4.14 Energy Consumption of MAODV, ODMRP, PDTMRP and C-MRP

Table 4.13 Energy Consumption of MAODV, ODMRP, PDTMRP and C-MRP

Simulation Time (ms)	Energy Consumption (J)			
	MAODV	ODMRP	PDTMRP	C-MRP
0	0	0	0	0
10	0.152469	0.136428	0.082366	0.084535
20	0.155985	0.127527	0.089346	0.090626
30	0.169070	0.146329	0.099346	0.105565
40	0.178374	0.156874	0.125625	0.114555
50	0.188745	0.166834	0.134623	0.115545
60	0.189645	0.167853	0.136645	0.123351
70	0.189645	0.167853	0.136645	0.123351
80	0.189645	0.167853	0.136645	0.123351
90	0.189645	0.167853	0.136645	0.123351
100	0.189645	0.167853	0.136645	0.123351

Figure 4.14 and Table 4.13 confirm that the energy acquired by the proposed OTP is 26 % greater than MAODV, 7 % higher than ODMRP and 5% superior to PDTMRP protocols. Thus, the performance of the proposed C-MRP is inferred to be better over all other existing protocols and energy confirms its efficiency and helps to extend the life time of the underlying network topology to certain extent.

4.8 PERFORMANCE ANALYSIS

The review of a routing protocol typically depends on measuring various routing metrics of a network such as PDR, PLR, delay time, and energy consumption.

4.8.1 Packet Delivery Ratio

The PDR values obtained from the two works proposed in this research work are plotted and compared against existing protocols in Figure 4.15.

Table 4.14 Comparison of PDR

Simulation Time (ms)	Packet Delivery Ratio (%)					
	OTP_F	OTP_H	E-COPS	AGDA	FBORP	C-MRP
0	0	0	0	0	0	0
10	0.957	0.949	0.91	0.748	0.63	0.954
20	0.93	0.967	0.82	0.719	0.61	0.977
30	0.92	0.969	0.81	0.727	0.601	0.987
40	0.909	0.974	0.791	0.719	0.602	0.988
50	0.911	0.929	0.824	0.72	0.601	0.989
60	0.94	0.986	0.827	0.709	0.602	0.991
70	0.92	0.989	0.86	0.723	0.601	0.993
80	0.919	0.988	0.815	0.719	0.603	0.995
90	0.925	0.993	0.82	0.719	0.605	0.997
100	0.92	0.994	0.817	0.72	0.606	0.997

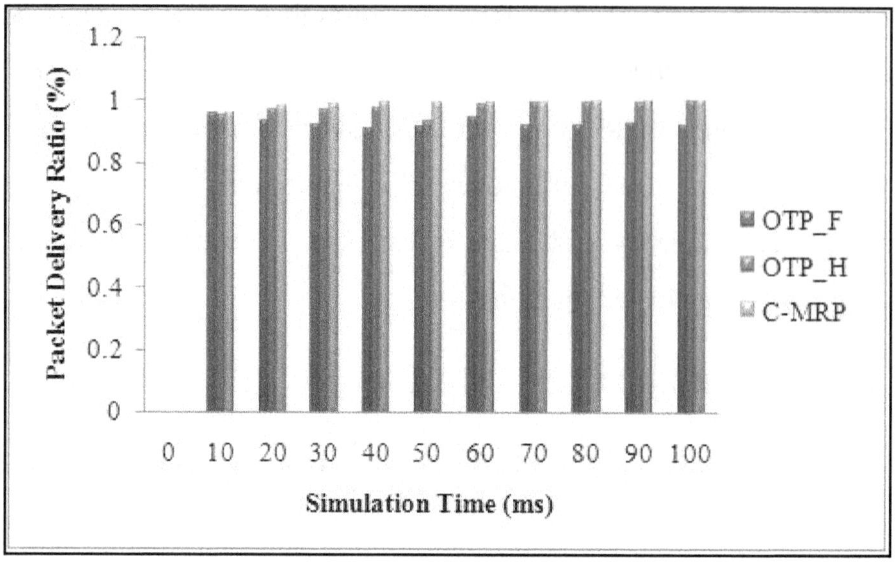

Figure 4.15 Evaluation of PDR results

Figure 4.15 indicates that the packet delivery ratio of C-MRP has been greater by integrating the proposed OTP than existing protocols found in the literature.

4.8.2 Packet Loss Ratio

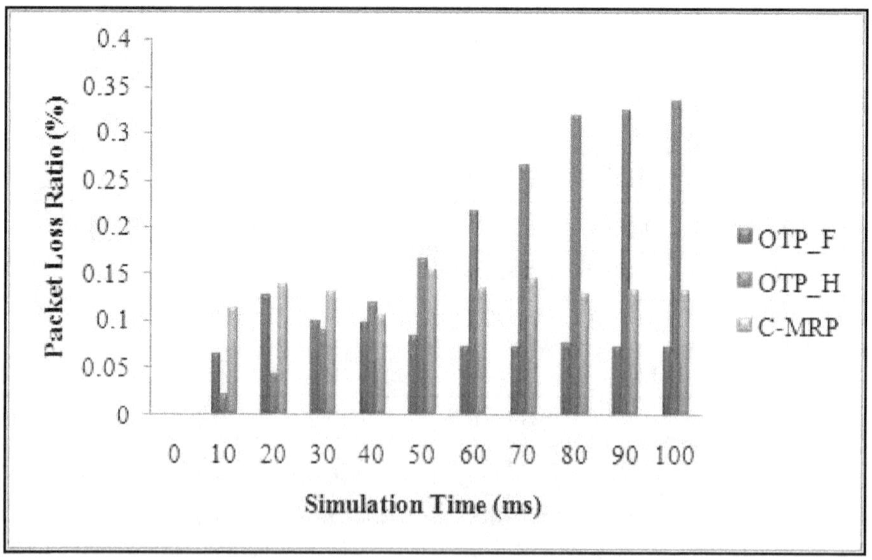

Figure 4.16 Evaluation of PLR results

The assessment of simulated PLR results of different protocols OTP, E-COPS, AGDA, FBORP and C-MRP are drawn in the Figure 4.16 and tabulated in Table 4.15 for detecting best among them. The overall packet lost caused by the FBROP looks is higher than all the other routing protocols. However, the proposed C-MRP has caused only minimum packet lost. Thus, the C-MRP is well suited for real-time critical applications.

Table 4.15 Comparison of PLR

Simulation Time (ms)	Packet Loss Ratio (%)					
	OTP_F	OTP_H	E-COPS	AGDA	FBORP	C-MRP
0	0	0	0	0	0	0
10	0.064	0.0211	0.241	0.258	0.253	0.113
20	0.125	0.0423	0.187	0.287	0.321	0.138
30	0.098	0.088	0.186	0.295	0.352	0.129
40	0.097	0.1175	0.188	0.293	0.365	0.105
50	0.082	0.1643	0.173	0.286	0.36	0.153
60	0.072	0.2163	0.189	0.285	0.36	0.134
70	0.071	0.2652	0.257	0.288	0.36	0.143
80	0.075	0.3174	0.189	0.288	0.363	0.128
90	0.072	0.3245	0.189	0.289	0.363	0.132
100	0.072	0.3342	0.187	0.289	0.363	0.131

4.8.3 Delay

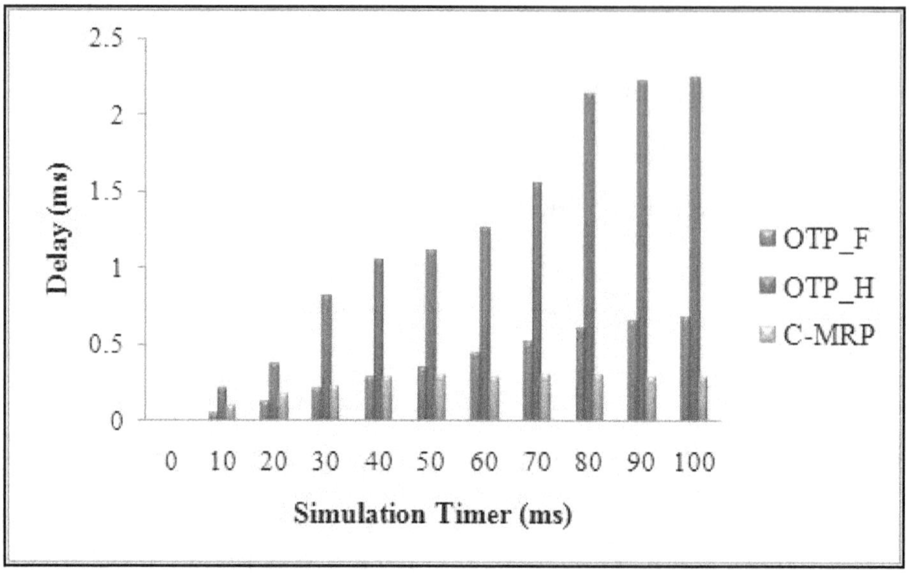

Figure 4.17 Comparison of Delay

Table 4.16 Comparison of Delay time

Simulation Time (ms)	Delay (ms)					
	OTP_F	OTP_H	E-COPS	AGDA	FBORP	C-MRP
0	0	0	0	0	0	0
10	0.0481	0.2101	0.0643	0.1242	0.326125	0.1
20	0.1219	0.3674	0.1784	0.3246	0.673975	0.17
30	0.2012	0.8103	0.2642	0.5242	1.262685	0.22
40	0.2753	1.044	0.3641	0.7255	1.533155	0.28
50	0.3461	1.113	0.4544	0.9371	1.900175	0.29
60	0.4353	1.2521	0.5354	1.2477	2.369972	0.28
70	0.5156	1.5564	0.6301	1.5171	2.478975	0.29
80	0.6021	2.1329	0.7245	1.5173	2.927072	0.29
90	0.6516	2.2163	0.8364	1.7199	3.343758	0.28
100	0.6721	2.2454	0.9014	1.9986	3.586775	0.28

The delay time of various protocols including the proposed OTP and C-MRP is measured through simulation and tabulated in Table 4.16. In addition, a pictorial plot of Table 4.16 is plotted as a graph in Figure 4.17 to strongly justify the performance of various routing protocols. Figure 4.17 shows that the FBROP takes the maximum delay in contrast to all other routing protocols but the proposed C-MRP takes only minimum delay time for routing data between a sender node and its destination node. This implies that the C-MRP is more suitable for time constrained real-time applications ofMANETs.

4.8.4 Energy Consumption

The Energy Consumption metric is typically a separate design issue of MANETs, however it critically affects the entire performance of the underlying current network topology and helps to improve the life time of the network. Thus evaluating the energy requirement of different protocols becomes one of the contributions of this research work. Various protocols like OTP under flat and hierarchical networks, E-COPS, AGDA, and FBROP have been compared as shown in Table 4.17 and Figure 4.18.

Table 4.17 Comparison of Delay time

	Energy Consumption (J)				
Simulation Time (ms)	**OTP**	**E-COPS**	**AGDA**	**FBORP**	**C-MRP**
0	0	0	0	0	0
10	0.0102	0.013494	0.0124	0.011502	0.0845
20	0.0121	0.016727	0.0143	0.014378	0.0906
30	0.0131	0.021087	0.016	0.017843	0.1056
40	0.0154	0.026524	0.0177	0.021308	0.1146
50	0.0175	0.02734	0.0205	0.024773	0.1155
60	0.0211	0.032411	0.023	0.027238	0.1234
70	0.0206	0.035721	0.0249	0.030203	0.1234
80	0.0224	0.038388	0.0262	0.033168	0.1234
90	0.0242	0.043782	0.0281	0.035633	0.1234
100	0.0258	0.044462	0.0309	0.039098	0.1234

It has been observed that the energy consumed while transmitting either data packets or control packets by both the proposed OTP and C-MRP is moderately low compared to all other existing protocols found in the literature. This indicates that the proposed C-MRP ensures minimal dissipation of energy required during routing packets. Figure 4.18 points out that the C-MRP mechanism that relies on fuzzy rules requires low energy consumption during routing packets because of the incorporated novel route discovery algorithm.

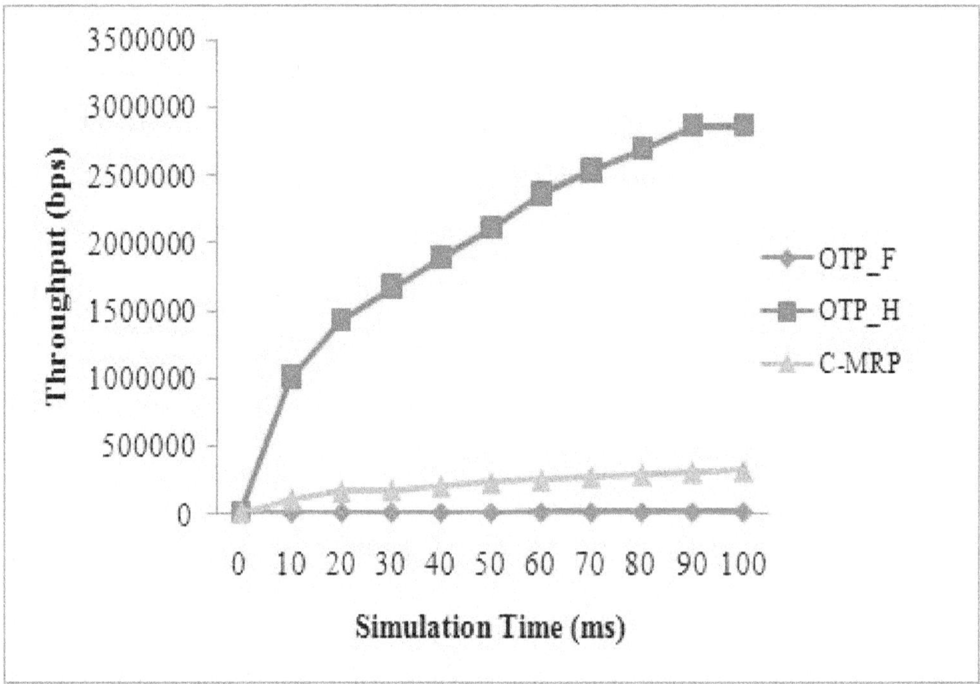

Figure 4.18 Comparison of Energy Consumption

4.8.5 Throughput

The overall performance of the network routing protocol being proposed depends on the total amount of throughput achieved. Table 4.18 shows different values of the throughput attained by OTP, E-COPS, AGDA, FBROP, and C-MRP protocols.

Table 4.18 Simulation time vs Throughput

Simulation Time (ms)	Throughput (bps)					
	OTP_F	OTP_H	E-COPS	AGDA	FBORP	C-MRP
0	0	0	0	0	0	0
10	235	999845	334.382	283.462	187.704	102431
20	989	1423462	699.588	591.544	510.77	158265
30	1533	1667347	1043.27	966.676	734.687	168290
40	2259	1878984	1423.11	1201.11	1016.46	198896
50	2890	2109374	1755.75	1590.24	1305.84	225629
60	3577	2356920	2174.28	1923.67	1568.33	245475
70	4222	2525784	2475.63	2244.8	1832.3	268269
80	4770	2689290	2826.39	2566.74	2107.69	286286
90	5524	2859047	3112.12	2885.77	2368.97	303541
100	6028	2859234	3526.76	3184.69	2617.99	314587

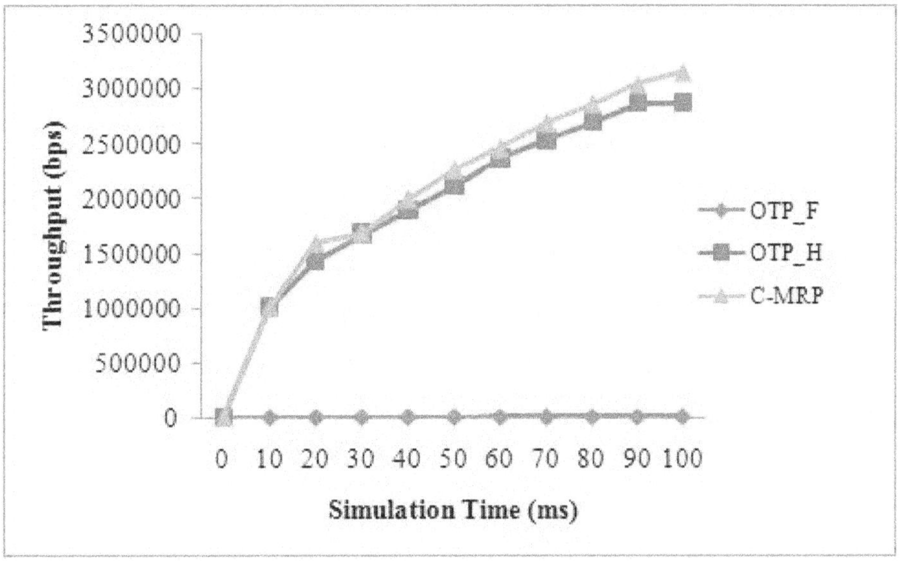

Figure 4.19 Throughput Consumption

The throughput obtained for different protocols are depicted in Figure 4.19. By comparing the proposed OTP and C-MRP against all other existing protocols, it is clear that the proposed OTP under flat network topology has achieved constant throughput but the proposed C-MRP has achieved greater throughput than all other protocols.

4.9 SUMMARY

In this chapter a cross-layer based optimized multicast route finding protocol and C-MRP in MANET based on fuzzy logic are proposed and developed. The key concept of the proposed C-MRP protocol is to determine the values of bandwidth and route stability of various mobile nodes which appear in multiple routes. Optimal route between nodes are determined by applying fuzzy logic system, fuzzification/Defuzzification process, and fuzzy logical decision system to solve the issues found in the open accessed freely available protocols. The proposed protocol overcomes the issues like route stability, increased packet deliver ratio, delay and minimal PDR value which are found in open accessed protocols. And also outperforms than existing protocols in all aspects and thus improves the life time of the network to certain extent.

Further, PDR, PLR, delay time, throughput and energy consumption of all the protocols including the proposed OTP and C-MRP are compared against each other. The key point of the proposed protocol is that it can be utilized for a particular real-time application based on its very strong features. However, the C-MRP method suits fine for time-critical applications in MANETs.

CHAPTER 5

IMPLEMENTATION OF CROSS LAYER BASED OPTIMIZED POWER UTILIZATION PROTOCOL FOR ROUTE DISCOVERY

Due to rapid changes in the topology of MANET, routing becomes more critical which leads to frequent link failure and so route change has to be performed often. Thus providing QoS for certain application will be challenging (Wu and Negi, 2003). When a link failure occurs, the route repair has to done either locally or a new route path should be discovered. The packets will be dropped when there is failure in the link. This will lead to the poor utilization of the network resources. In this chapter, AODVOPL protocol is proposed for link prediction to estimate the availability of active link to the neighbouring nodes. Based on this information, when link failure is expected between two nodes, proactively an alternate path is built up even before the link breaks. This reduces the data packet drops and hence the recovery time.

5.1 CROSS LAYER DESIGN

The function of the network is divided into several layers. The known protocol called OSI model has seven layers of protocol stack. These layers are arranged one above the other, to support the higher layer stack and to do its intended function.

In traditional network, packets are delivered using protocol header and the functions are carried out using the network model. In a stack model, each layer is assigned some specific task and provides service to upper layer in the protocol stack.

The traditional layered architecture is constructed in such a way that, the adjacent layers only can be communicated by the use of standard interface. This helps in blocking direct exchange of data between non adjacent layers.

Protocols can be designed, so that direct interactions are possible between non adjacent layers of the stack. The cross layer refers to the design that makes communication possible between non-adjacent layers in the protocol stack.

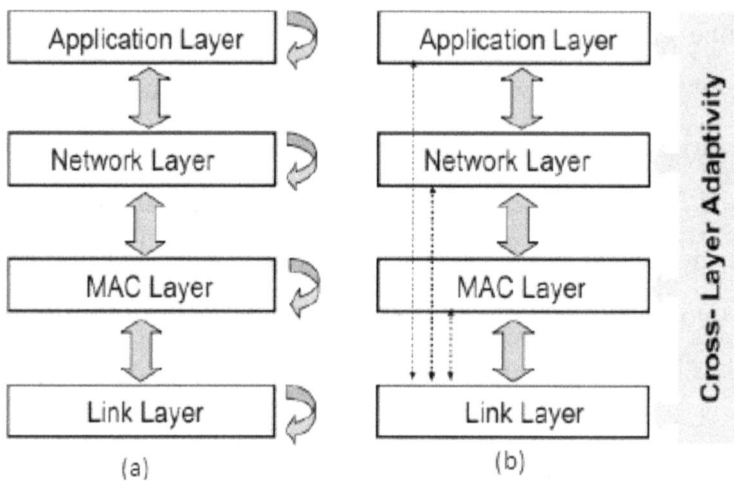

Figure 5.1LayeredandCross layered architecture

5.2 MOTIVATION FOR CROSS LAYER DESIGN

5.2.1 TCP on Wireless

The cross layer design helps in reducing the network congestion. A TCP sender wrongly suspects a packet error in a wireless link to be an indicator of network congestion. This can be avoided by direct interaction between link layer and transport layer.

5.2.2 Real-Time Multimedia on Wireless Links

When real-time data are transmitted through shared wireless links, the algorithm deployed at lower layer of the protocol stack need to be modified so that they get adapted with the algorithms employed at higher layer protocol stack model.

Due to the time varying tendency of the wireless link, complications like increased error probability and latency arises in multiple access over shared wireless link. To overcome the problem cross layer design approach is required.

5.2.3 Energy Efficiency

In wireless link, utilization of energy is a very important concern. Efficiency of energy of a communication device cannot be explained using any one of the layers in the protocol stack. The solution for the design problem of energy efficient, Ad Hoc network makes use of cross layer design architecture.

5.2.4 Power Control

The layers of the traditional layered architecture get affected due to the error prone wireless medium. In a network, if all nodes have high transmission power, there will be high interference probability so that nodes fail to communicate with in the network. This motivates to implement cross layered architecture.

5.3 METHODS OF CROSS LAYER DESIGN

This section describes about the various methods to implement the cross layer design. It elaborates how the communication happens between two non-adjacent layers in the protocol stack. Based on the literature survey, the data transfer between non-adjacent layers occurs by merging the adjacent layers, by providing interface between lower and higher layer stack and by modifying the boundaries of the layer.

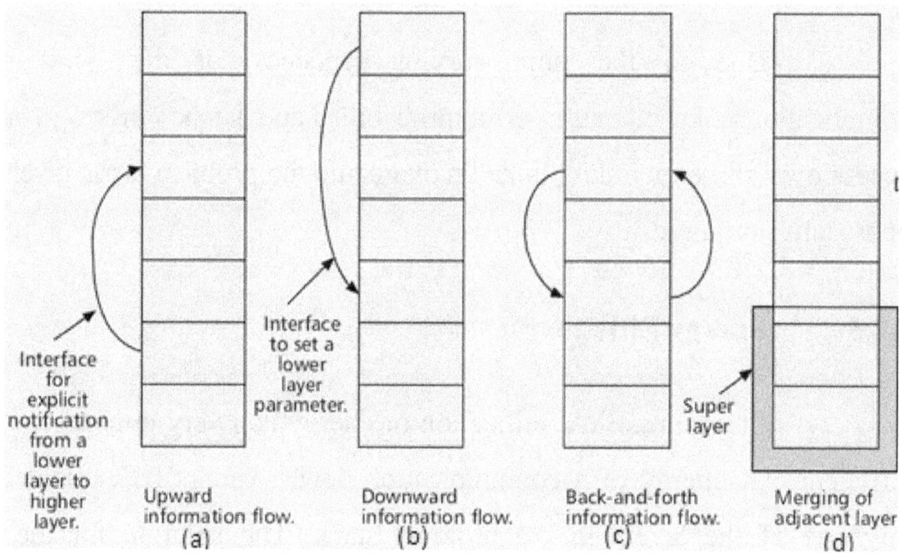

Figure 5.2 Methods of cross layer design

5.4 CROSS LAYER PROTOCOLS

The wireless medium in Ad Hoc network has limited resources. The nodes in the network are mobile, due to which the channel becomes unpredictable and dynamic. These factors influence to perform optimization using the data available at different layers of protocol stack. There are many cross layer solutions discussed in the literature.

In this section, four layers namely physical layer, MAC layer, Network layer and transport layers are considered for obtaining the cross layer solution.

5.4.1 Physical and Network Layer Interaction

The difference in performance of physical layer when compared with cross layer design is studied in (Chellappa and Pan2002). Path loss and shadowing properties are used for comparing the results in DMR, LANMAR, LAR, RIP and ZRP protocols.

The author states that, while discovery of route in Ad Hoc network, the present state of the channel and link quality should be considered.

5.4.2 Physical and Transport Cross Layer Interactions

The data rate of the mobile nodes gets influenced by various reasons. One reason is that the data rate gets affected by the power with which the nodes transmit the data.

A distributive power control algorithm is proposed in Chiang (2005) balance the power and congestion control in physical and transport layer respectively. This algorithm helps in enhancing the network performance by maintaining the stability and robustness.

5.4.3 MAC and Transport Cross Layer Interactions

The loss of packets in a network may be due to various factors. Fluctuations in the wireless link, node mobility, congestion in the network are a few factors that affect packet loss. The TCP is unable to distinguish the packet loss due to congestion in the network and to other factors. This leads to poor performance of TCP in Ad Hoc networks.

The cross-layer congestion control scheme is proposed in(KliazovichandGranelli2006) gives higher performance by gathering capacity information such as bandwidth and delay at the link layer. This paper solves the problem by modifying the MAC or the TCP in isolation and some solutions explore joint strategies at MAC and TCP layers.

5.5 CROSS LAYER OPTIMIZATION PROTOCOL

This chapter proposes a cross layer design for optimized power utilization protocol and link availability prediction. This algorithm helps in increasing the battery life of the Ad Hoc nodes and also predicts the availability of the links efficiently. In traditional wireless network, a change in path between nodes is required when there is failure in the link or when a shortest path is found between nodes. The failure in the link between nodes is found by observing multiple retransmission timeouts. This leads to delay in restoring the link between nodes.

To overcome this problem, link availability prediction algorithm is proposed that predicts the time after which the link may fail. The link prediction is done by measuring the power of the data packets at the receiver. If the received power of the data packets is less than the threshold value, the proposed algorithm detects that link failure is going to occur and alerts the source node to find a new path.

The link failure is predicted using (Jiang, 2001). In this method signal strength of four consecutive data packets transmitted by the predecessor are measured to predict the link failure.

The receiver maintains a record of time at which the data packets are received and also the received signal power of the recent four data packets. For instance let us assume that a receiver node receives four data packets at time t_1, t_2, t_3 and t_4 with signal power of P_1, P_2, P_3 and P_4 respectively. With the help of threshold signal power P_t, the time at which the link may fail t_p can be predicted. The threshold signal power P_t, is chosen in such a way that the receiver is able to receive data packets with minimum signal power.

The routing protocol to be deployed needs some time to find a new path which is referred as critical time t_c. The critical time t_c should be sufficient for the receiver to send link error message to the transmitter node so that it can react and find a new link for data transmission.

The critical time should be smaller than link break time. After time t_c, the node enters into critical state and should find an alternate route. When a link is expected to fail between nodes, the upstream node first attempts to find a route to the destination. If such route is not found within a fixed time called discovery period, a link failure warning is sent towards the sources whose flows are using this link. Source nodes can invoke the route discovery mechanism to setup restoration paths. At time, the received power is sufficient for sending warning message to the upstream node and discovering an alternate path either by local route repair around the link which is going to break or by setting up new paths from sources. As two nodes move outwards, signal power of the nodes drop. Thus we define link break when nodes are first crossing the radio transmission range and broken links are repaired locally in k hops. The value of k is two, i. e., broken links can be repaired in two hops. The proposed local route repair procedure attempts to repair broken route locally with minimum control overheads for faster recovery.

Table 5.1 AODV optimized power utilization and link prediction algorithm

Procedure

```
        If (P1>P2 )∩(P2>P3)∩(P3>P4) then use Prediction (),
        Prediction ()
        {
        before link fails, predict and update tp and tc
        }
        If (present time ≥tc )
        {
        receiver sends a beacon to the source node,
        to make hibernate for predefined time interval.
        }
        After getting the repair information,
        Make the status of the link and route is going to fail soon
        Local route repair().
        {
        Discover new data path to the immediate next node;
        If path is found within k hops and the stipulated time
        Fix the path for data transmission.
        Else
        Rediscover new data path to receiver D;
        If (path is found)
        {
        Start transmitting the packets via rediscovered path,
        Make the source to identify path using shortest distance method.
        }
}
        for every adjacent node,
        Once data packets being received,
Receiver fill in the record of the last four data packets signal strength and time of reception
        At source
        {
        New path discover message received,
        Discover new path,
        Redirect traffic through new path.
        }
```

5.6 SIMULATION RESULTS

We have simulated AODV routing algorithm and with AODVOPL to determine performance. NS-2 has been used for this purpose. At the MAC layer, IEEE 802.11 protocol is used for simulation.

The performance of the model is evaluated in terms of number of route failures, packet delivery ratio and average end-to-end delay as a function of number of nodes and node mobility.

5.6.1 Packet Delivery Ratio

The ratio between the client of packages originated by the "application layer" of constant bit rate sources and the number of packages received by the constant bit rate receiver at the final destination:

$$Packet\ Delivery\ Ratio = \frac{Number\ of\ packets\ received}{Number\ of\ packets\ transmitted} \quad (5.1)$$

5.6.2 Average End-To-End Delay

This is the common wait between the delivering of the information bundle by the CBR resource and its invoice at the corresponding CBR recipient.

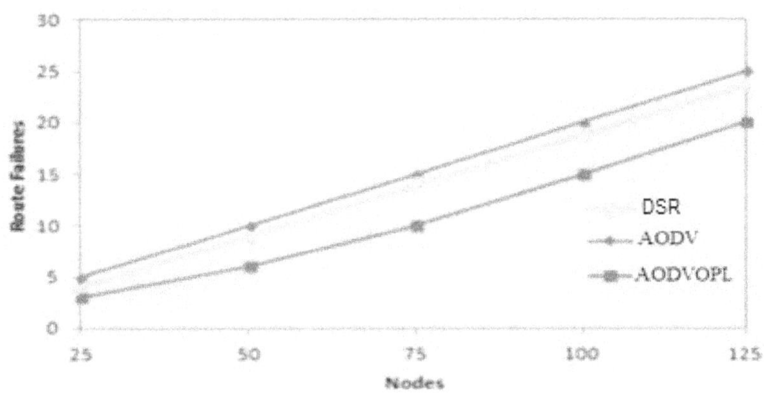

Figure 5.3 Nodes vs Route failure

Figure 5.3 shows the variation in the route failures with increasing network size. Results show that route failures are much less in AODVOPL as compared to AODV and DSR. It is due to that AODVOPL, searches for new routes in prior to the link failure, and messages are delivered through the new route.

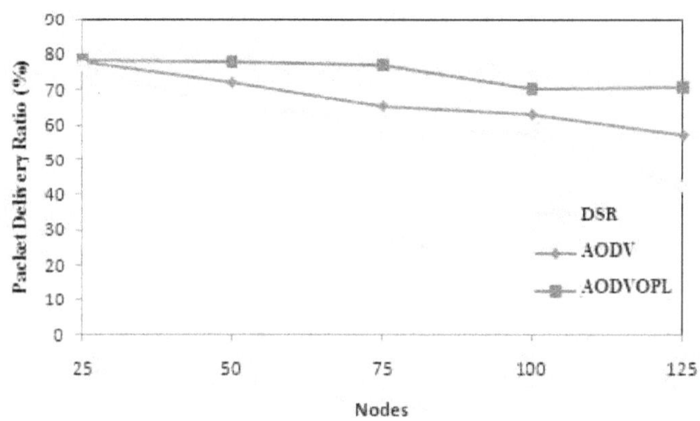

Figure 5.4 Packet Delivery Ratio vs Nodes

Figure 5.4 shows that packet delivery ratio increases with increase in the network size. Results show that packet delivery ratio is better in AODVOPL as compared to AODV and DSR. It is due to the factor that AODVOPL finds the alternative routes before the link fails and hence data packets are successfully delivered to the intended destination.

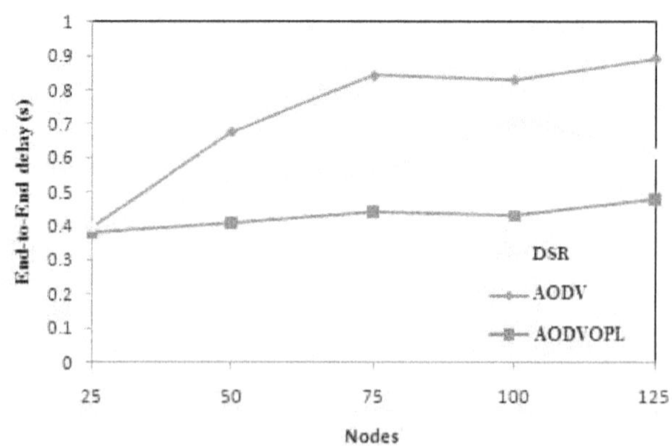

Figure 5.5 End-to-end delay vs Nodes

Figure 5.5 shows that end-to-end delay in AODVOPL is much lesser when compared with AODV and DSR. This is due to prior route discovery when the link fails. When the number of nodes is increased in the network, end-to-end delay of AODVOPL, AODV and DSR increases. This is mainly because of collisions in the network, which result in retransmission of packets.

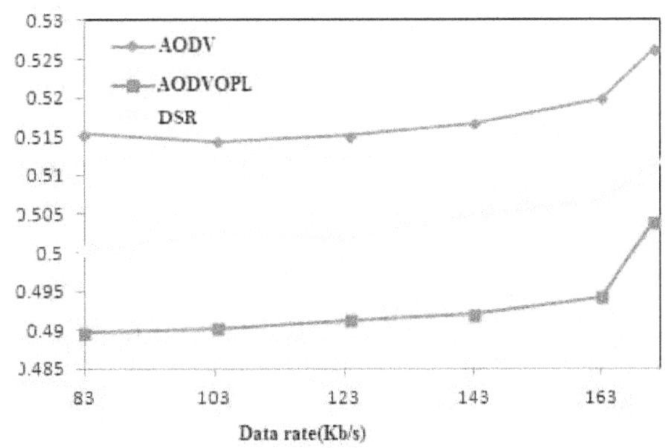

Figure 5.6 Energy consumption vs Data rate

Figure 5.6 shows the amount of energy consumed per successful packet transmission with increasing packet data rate. Results show that energy consumption is lesser in AODVOPL as compared to AODV and DSR. It is due to the reduced packet drop in AODVOPL and thus, avoiding retransmissions of packets.

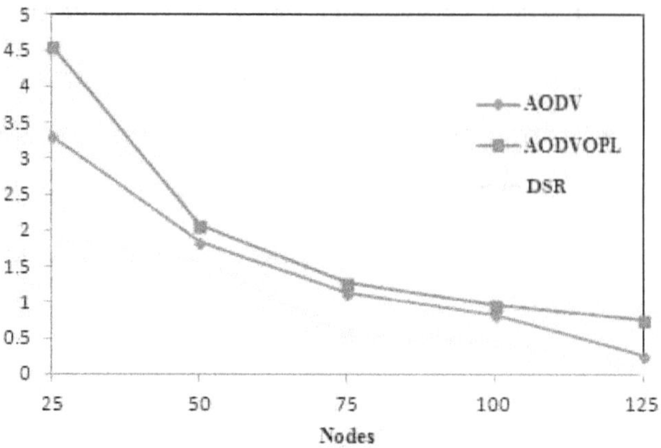

Figure 5.7 Throughput vs Nodes

Figure 5.7 shows that in AODV, AODVOPL and DSR the throughput is decreasing with increase in number of nodes. This is because increase in node density increases traffic that leads to collision.

5.7 SUMMARY

In this chapter, AODV routing protocol with optimized power and link prediction for Ad Hoc networks is discussed. A prediction algorithm is implemented that predicts link failure by the knowledge of signal strength of the four consecutive received packets and threshold signal strength. The proposed protocol can thus initiate the new route finding process even before the occurrence of failure.

The performance of the proposed AODVOPL has been evaluated and compared with AODV using simulations. The simulation results show that the proposed algorithm out performs and results in lower end-to-end delay and higher packet delivery ratio.

CHAPTER 6

IMPLEMENTATION OF CROSS LAYER USING POWER OPTIMIZATION AND LINK AVAILABILITY PREDICTION PROTOCOL

Frequent changes in network topology due to mobility and limited battery power of the mobile devices are the key challenges in the mobile adhoc networks. The depletion of power source may cause early unavailability of nodes and thus links in the network. The mobility of nodes causes frequent routes breaks and adversely affects the required performance of the applications.

In MANETs, a node performs its task with battery power. The availability of battery power tends to change for the nodes deployed in a network. The nodes are mobile and hence the link between source and destination may fail. Thus providing QoS with highly unpredictable links need prior routing recovery, along with transport and application layer optimization.

In order to be mobile, unmetered connectivity using wireless interfaces need to be present with every node in the network. Usually mobile nodes will depend on battery power for their operations. It is desirable to minimize the power consumption in these nodes. Further, this problem is important as once the battery of the node is exhausted, it cannot transmit as well as receive any data. It dies resulting in impact on network connectivity since in adhoc networks, even intermediate nodes are important to maintain connectivity. As soon as one of the intermediate nodes dies, the whole link has to be formed again. This leads to large amount of delay, waste of scarce node resources like battery power thereby hampering the throughput of the whole system. Further, mobility presents the challenges in the form of continuously variable topology and thus requiring a complex and energy efficient routing mechanisms. Wireless networks will be used mostly by personal communication devices which people can carry with them. These small, always connected personal devices will lead to new applications. For running most of these applications on resource limited devices, one needs efficient networking stack in the mobile devices. Conventionally to simplify the complex task of handling network connectivity, layered architecture had been used. To further improve the performance, the concept of layered software components is now being broken by also allowing layers to access data structures from non-immediate layers. This approach is popularly known as cross layer optimization.

In this chapter, a cross layer design for power optimization and link availability prediction (POLAP) protocol are proposed for mobile Ad Hoc networks that provide solution for power optimization and link availability.

It improves the throughput, packet delivery ratio by prior prediction of link breaks and initiating the route repair. It also reduces communication interruption time, routing overheads, end-to end delay and power consumption by use of cross layer interaction.

The simulation results show that the proposed cross layer design improves the throughput, packet delivery ratio by prior prediction of link failure and initiating the route repair.

6.1 POWER OPTIMIZATION AND LINK AVAILABILITY PREDICTION (POLAP)

Cross layer based method POLAP increases the nodes lifetime by optimizing the power in transmitting RTS, CTS, DATA and ACK packets. Also estimation of link availability, discovery of link prior to its failure is performed to provide the Quality of Service (QoS).In this approach, the signal strength of the received packet is obtained from the physical layer and is sent to the MAC layer for further transmission. The optimum transmit power is computed using equation (6.1).

$$P_{optimum} \geq \frac{P_{thresh} * P_t' * C}{P_r'} \tag{6.1}$$

Where, $P_{optimum}$ is the optimum power with which the packet has to be transmitted, P_t is the transmit power of the packet, P_r is the received power of the packet, P_t' is the transmitted power of the previous packet, P_r' is the received power of the previous packet, and C is constant for compensation of interference in the network.The optimum power value is updated at each node in the table against the destination. In order to get the optimum transmit power in the cross layer design, the header fields of packets RTS, CTS, DATA and ACK are modified to incorporate the transmit power level of the respective packets.

6.1.1 Proposed Algorithm

Table 6.1 Power optimization and Link availability prediction at transmitter

Line	Procedure
1	At transmitter:
2	Let $P_t = 2.818$
	optimum power table at the transmitter node for the receiver node address and its stored optimum transmit power value
3	If node entry is available, then else ,
4	Append power value in RTS header and send RTS with this power,
5	Receive CTS packet; observe its received power and extract transmit power.
6	The node calculates optimum transmit power for DATA packet,
7	Update optimum power table,
8	Add the power level in the DATA packet header and send the DATA packet at optimum transmit power level,
9	Receive ACK,
10	End.

Table 6.2 Power optimization and Link availability prediction at receiver

Procedure

At receiver:
Everyneighbor node,
When a packet is received,
If (P_r>P_t,then Power optimization()
Else
{
Receiver updatespower and time of reception of recentfour packets,
If and (P_1>P_2),(P_2>P_3) and (P_3>P_4) then Prediction (),
Prediction ()
{
Estimate and change the t_p and t_c, prior to link failure
}
If (current time >= t_c)
{
Beacon is sent to source node,
Not allowing further transmission of packets.
}
On reception of service information packet,
Make the status the route and link soontobe failed,
}
Power optimization ()
{
Receive RTS,
Note the receive power and calculate the optimum transmit power for the CTS packet. Update optimum transmit power table with power level ,
Insert the optimum transmit power in the CTS header and send the CTS packet at the same power level,
Receive DATA packet,
Include the optimum power level in the ACK packet header and send the ACK packet at this transmit power level,
}
End.
 	
At source:
{
New path discover message received,
Discover new path,
Redirect traffic through new path.
}

6.2 SIMULATION AND RESULTS

Table 6.3 Simulation Parameters for POLAP Protocol

Traffic Pattern	Constant Bit Rate
Simulation Time	900 seconds
Total Connections	20, 25, 30, 35, 40, 45 and 50
Packet size	512 Bytes
Velocity	5, 10, 15, 20, 25 and 30 meters/second
Pause Time	10 seconds
Simulation Area	1500m by 300m
Total Nodes	25, 50, 75, 100 and 125

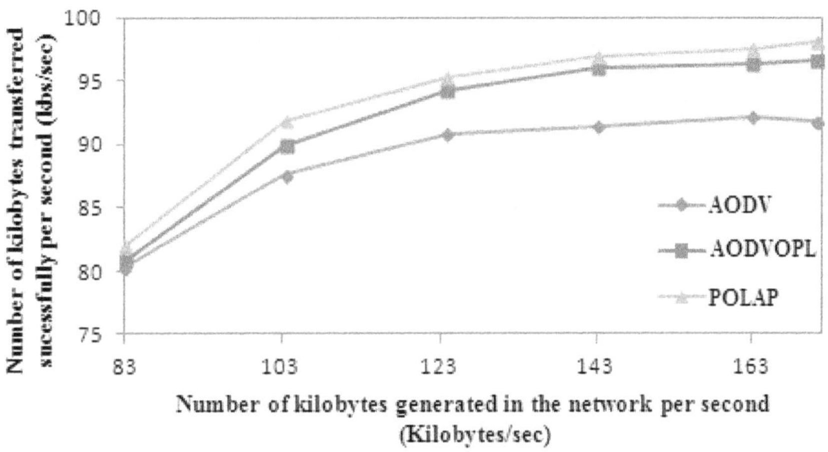

Figure 6.1 Throughput vs packet generation rate

Figure 6.1 shows throughput of AODV, AODVOPL and POLAP. It is clear that POLAP produce increased throughput compared to AODVOPL and AODV (Azad*et al.* 2007) protocols. It is due to POLAP uses smaller carrier sensing range compared to AODVOPL and AODV, therefore large number of nodes can be transmitted simultaneously.

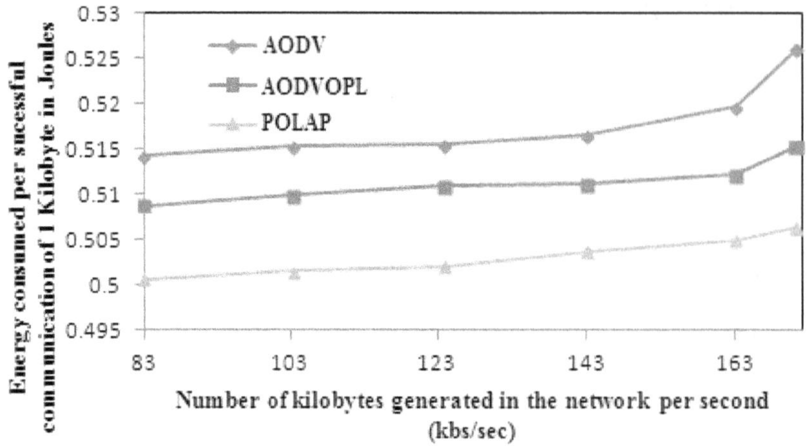

Figure 6.2 Energy consumption Vs packet generation rate

Figure 6.2 shows variation of energy consumed per successful communication with increase in packet generation rate. Results show that power is low in POLAP as compared to AODVOPL and AODV. POLAP consumes less power as compared to other schemes as it uses low power for communication of RTS, CTS, DATA and ACK packets and link successes are also observed and avoiding retransmissions of packets. However, POLAP, AODVOPL and AODV give increasing average energy consumption as network load increases.

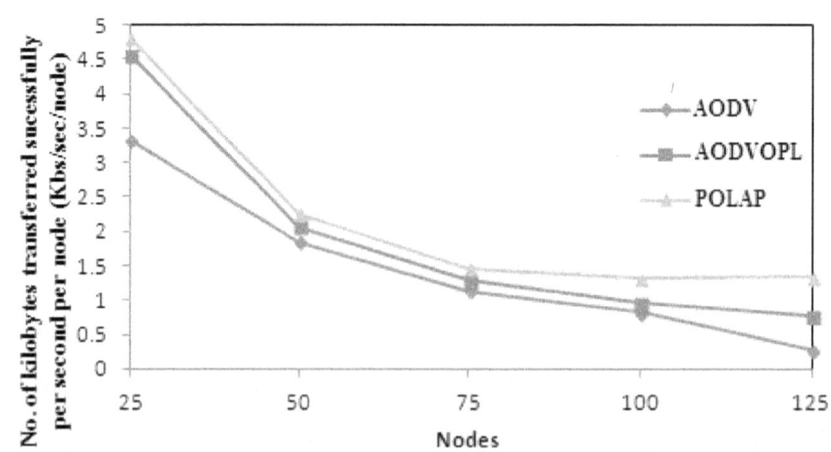

Figure 6.3 Number of Nodes Vs Throughput per node

Figure 6.3 shows that the throughput per node is best in POLAP as compared to AODVOPL and AODV. This happens because in POLAP scheme, concurrent transmission occur due to the use of optimum transmit power which is lesser as well as proactive route discovery used during route failures and thus delivering more data. The throughput per node is decreasing in all the schemes with increase in number of nodes because this increases collision.

6.3 SUMMARY

The performance of the proposed cross layer design for the power optimization protocol and link prediction perform well as compared to AODVOPL and AODV, this results in better throughput, lower energy consumption thus longer battery life and better delivered network because of lowest overhead routing packets and average interruption time due to the use of optimum (lower) transmit power and prior route repair processes. Therefore, it improves networks and nodes lifetime and capacity to support quality-of-service.

CHAPTER 7

CONCLUSIONS AND FUTURE RESEARCH WORK

This chapter finally concludes the thesis work with a concise discussion on the merits and demerits of the developed algorithms and techniques for discovering optimal multicast routes in MANET. In addition, a few open issues in the decisive area of research work are also revealed.

7.1 CONCLUSIONS

Developing a multicast optimal routing scheme for MANETs, which supports mobility of mobile nodes is a challenging problem, because of energetic change in the accessible network topology and constrained resources. The vital information in a protocol that supports a cross-layer method flows between two different layers directly and instantly. However, different layers of a MANET may compete for the active resources simultaneously. Though there were many algorithms and protocols proposed in the past, each protocol has its own advantages and limitation. In addition, the literature survey exposes that energy optimization techniques are not sufficient to improve the life-time of an Ad Hoc network. Therefore, designing an energy efficient protocol for MANETs is very important for time critical real-time applications.

In this thesis, an optimal route detection algorithm and cross-layer based multicasting protocol that extends the life-time of the underlying network have been proposed. The developed protocol is evaluated and assessed by conducting various simulation experiments by using NS2 tool.

A multicasting algorithm, namely, OTP has been proposed and developed for detecting optimal and energy efficient routes between a source node and the destination node in a MANET. The OTP approach discovers energy optimized route based on the relative angle of an intermediate node and its available energy.

This thesis work finally proposed a cross-layer based multicast route discovery protocol, namely, C-MRP, a cross layer based optimized multicast route finding protocol that uses fuzzy logical decision method for MANETs. The route stability between two adjacent mobile nodes are predicted using its link quality. Also, the source mobile node makes use of fuzzification procedure for discovering optimal path.

The proposed optimized route finding protocol relies on fuzzy linguistic decision rule set to offer reliable data communication and minimizing the computational overhead when the network load is heavy, increasing packet throughput ratio, minimizing delay and PLR, and improving the life time of the network.

Experimental results confirm that C-MRP produces better result in all aspects than all existing solutions discussed in Chapter 2. The proposed C-MRP outperforms than the existing solutions proposed by Basarkod*et al.* (2014), Zhu *et al.*(2004) and Young-jun*et al.* (2017).with the energy consumption of 1- 3 percent which helps to improve the life time of the overall network topology.

Further the thesis proposes cross layer design based power optimization and link availability prediction algorithm. The result of the proposed protocol is compared with AODV and AODVOPL protocol. This results in better throughput, lower energy consumption thus longer battery life and better delivered network because of lowest overhead routing packets and average interruption time due to use of optimum (lower) transmit power and prior route repair processes. Therefore, it improves networks and nodes lifetime and capacity to support quality-of-service.

The quintessence of this research lies in prediction of link before it fails, route recognition and better intermediate node selection during transmission of data packets from source to destination in MANETs through fuzzy logic system.

7.2 FUTURE RESEARCH WORKS

In this research work, some efforts are made to present solutions for discovering an optimal multicast route in MANETs by implementing a fuzzy logic based rule system. The presented protocol in this thesis work can be advanced as discussed follows.

- To support security services during multicast data communication through distribution mechanism.
- To implement a novel clustering algorithm together with mobility administration in OTP and C-MRP and EAARC to support scalability and ease of an energy efficient route detection.
- A mechanism to detect device duplication in MANETs because of the inclusion of several devices becomes a primary element of Internet of Things.
- Performance of link prediction routing can be evaluated for real-time traffic.
- Other power optimization protocol may be integrated to improve the performance of the network.

- The cross layer integration can also be included for other layers to further optimize the performance of the networks further.
- A lot of research can also be done in the other layers of the protocol stack. Therefore this study can be extended to design protocols with other schemes to achieve improved efficiency.

REFERENCES

1. Alireza Shams Shafigh, Kamran AbdollahiandMarjanKouchaki. 2012, 'Developing a Fuzzy Logic Based on Demand Multicast Routing Protocol', Journal of Electrical and Computer Engineering, Article ID. 389812, pp. 1-14.

2. Basarkod.P.I. and Sunilkumar S. Manvi. 2014, 'On-demand QoS and Stability Based Multicast Routing in Mobile Ad Hoc Networks', Journal of telecommunications and information technology, vol. 3, pp. 98-112.

3. Basu, P, Khan, N and Little, TDC. 2001, 'A mobility based metric for clustering in mobile ad hoc networks', In Proceedings of the international workshop on wireless networks and mobile computing (WNMC2001), pp. 16-19.

4. BhabaniSankar Gouda, Rabindra Kumar Shial, K Hemant K Reddy, 2012, 'An optimal Path Finding Routing Protocol for Mobile Adhoc Network Using Random Mobility Model', In Proceedings 2012 International Conference on Emerging Trends in Science, Engineering and Technology (INCOSET 2012), pp. 10-15.

5. Biswas, J andNandy, SK 2004, 'Application layer multicasting for mobile ad-hoc networks with network layer support', In Proceedings of the 29th Annual IEEE International Conference on Local Computer Networks (LCN '04), pp. 24-31.

6. Boukerche, A, Turgt, B, Aydin, N, Ahmad, MZ, Boloni, I andTurgut, D 2011, 'Routing Protocols in Ad Hoc Networks: A Survey', Computer Networks, vol. 55, no. 13, pp. 3032-3080.

7. C.SivaRam Murthy, B.S. Manoj, 2002, 'Ad Hoc Wireless Networks Architectures and Protocols', Prentice Hall, ISBN : 013147023X, ch. 5-11.

8. Cai, S and Yang, X 2003, 'The performance of pool ODMRP protocol', In Proceedings of the IFIP/IEEE International Conference on Management of Multimedia Networks and Services (MMNS '03), vol. 2839, pp. 90-101.

9. Cai, S, Yang, X and Yao, W 2003, 'The comparison between PoolODMRP and PatchODMRP', In Proceedings of the IEEE International Conference on Networks (ICON '03), pp. 729-735.

10. Cai, S, Yao, N, Wang, N, Yao, W andGu, G 2006, 'Multipath passive data acknowledgement on-demand multicast protocol', Computer Communications, vol. 29, no. 11, pp. 2074-2083.

11. Chang, JH andTassiulas, L 2000, 'Energy conserving routing in wireless ad-hoc networks' In Proceedings of the Conference on Computer Communications (IEEE Infocom 2000), pp. 22-31.

12. Chao Yang, Yuli Fu, Yan Zhang, ShengliXie, Rong Yu, 2013, 'Energy Efficient Hybrid Spectrum Access Scheme in Cognitive Vehicular Adhoc Networks', IEEE Communication Letters, vol. 17, Issue 2, pp. 329-332.

13. Charles E Perkins andPravinBhagwat 2000, 'DSDV: Routing over a Multihop Wireless Network of Mobile Computers', Technical report, IBM Research and University of Maryland, USA.

14. Chellappa, R and Pan, L 2006, 'A case for cross layer design : The impact of physical layer properties on routing protocol performance in MANETs', In Proceedings of Australian Telecommunication Networks and Applications Conference, pp. 409-413.

15. Chen, B, Jamieson, K, Morris, R andBalakrishnan, H 2001, 'Span: an energy-efficient coordination algorithm for topology maintenance in ad hoc wireless networks', In Proceedings of International Conference on Mobile Computing and Networking (MobiCom'2001), pp. 85-96.

16. Chen, K andNahrstedt, K 2002, 'Effective location-guided tree construction algorithms for small group multicast in MANET', In Proceedings of the Annual Joint Conference of the IEEE Computer and Communications Societies (INFOCOM'02), vol. 3, pp. 1180-1189.

17. Chen, X and Wu, J 2003, 'Multicasting techniques in mobile ad hoc networks', In The Handbook of Ad Hoc Wireless Networks, pp. 25-40.

18. Chiang, CC 1998, 'Wireless network multicasting', Ph.D. dissertation, Department of Computer Science, University of California, Los Angeles, Calif, USA.

19. Chiang, CC, Gerla, M and Zhang, L 1997, 'Shared tree wireless network multicast, In Proceedings of the 6th International Conference on Computer Communications and Networks (ICCCN '97), pp. 28-33.

20. Chiang, CC, Gerla, M and Zhang, L 1998, 'Adaptive shared tree multicast in mobile wireless networks', In Proceedings of the IEEE Global Telecommunications Conference (GLOBECOM '98), vol. 3, pp. 1817-1822.

21. Chiang, CC, Gerla, M and Zhang, L 1998, 'Forwarding Group Multicast Protocol (FGMP) for multihop, mobile wireless networks', ACM-Baltzer Journal of Cluster Computing, vol. 1, no. 2, pp. 187-196.

22. Chiang, M 2005, 'Balancing Transport and Physical Layers in Wireless Mutihop Networks: Jointly Optimal Congestion Control and Power Control', IEEE Journal on Selected Areas in Communications, vol. 23, no. 1, pp. 104-116.

23. Danny D Patel 2000, 'Energy in ad-hoc networking for the Pico Radio', Technical report.

24. Das, SK, Manoj, BS and Murthy, CSR 2002, 'A dynamic core based multicast routing protocol for ad hoc wireless networks', In Proceedings of the International Symposium on Mobile Ad Hoc Networking and Computing (MobiHoc '02), pp. 24-35.

25. Das, SK, Manoj, BS and Murthy, CSR 2002, 'Weight based multicast routing protocol for ad hoc wireless networks', In IEEE Global Telecommunications Conference (GLOBECOM '02), vol. 1, pp. 117-121.

26. Deering, S 1989, 'Host extensions for IP multicasting', http://www.ietf.org/rfc/rfc1112.txt.

27. De-Nian Yang, Wanjium Liao, 2008, 'Protocol Design for Scalable and Adaptive Multicast for Group Communications', In Proceedings of 2008 IEEE International Conference on Network Protocols, pp. 33-42.

28. DimitriosLiarokapis and Ali Shahrabi 2011, 'Fuzzy-based Probabilistic Broadcasting in Mobile Ad Hoc Networks', IEEE International Conference on Wireless Days (WD), IFIP, pp. 1-6.

29. Doshi, S, Bhandare, S and Brown, TX 2002, 'An on-demand minimum energy routing protocol for a wireless ad hoc network', Mobile Computing and Communications Review, vol. 6, no. 2, pp. 50-66.

30. DzmitryKliazovich andFabrizioGranelli, 2006, 'Cross-layer Congestion Control in Ad Hoc Wireless Networks', Journal on Ad Hoc Networks, vol. 4, no. 6, pp. 687-708.

31. Elizabeth M Royer and Chai-KeongToh 1999, 'A review of current routing protocols for ad hoc mobile wireless networks', Technical report, University of California and Georgia Institute of Technology, USA.

32. Eric Setton, TaesangYoo, Xiaoqing Zhu, Andrea Goldsmith and Bernd Girod 2005, 'Cross-Layer Design Of Ad Hoc Networks For Real-Time Video Streaming', IEEE Wireless Communications, vol. 12, no. 4, pp. 59-65.

33. Finn1987, 'Routing and Addressing Problems in Large Metropolitan-scale Internetworks', Technical Report ISI/RR-87-180, USC/ISI.

34. FotisFoukalas, Vangelis Gazisand NancyAlonistioti 2008, 'Cross-Layer Design Proposals for Wireless Mobile Networks: A Survey and Taxonomy', IEEE Communications Surveys and Tutorials, vol. 10, no. 1, pp. 70-85.

35. Garcia-Luna-Aceves, JJ andMadruga, EL 1999, 'The coreassisted mesh protocol', IEEE Journal on Selected Areas in Communications, vol. 17, no. 8, pp. 1380-1394.

36. Ge, M, Krishnamurthy, SV andFaloutsos, M 2006, 'Application versus network layer multicasting in ad hoc networks: the ALMA routing protocol', Ad Hoc Networks, vol. 4, no. 2, pp. 283-300.

37. Gerla, M, Chiang, CC and Zhang, L 1999, 'Tree multicast strategies in mobile, multihop wireless networks', ACM/Baltzer Journal on Mobile Networks and Application, vol. 4, no. 3, pp. 193-207.

38. Girling, G, Wa, J, Osborn, P andStefanova, R 1997, 'The design and implementation of a low power ad hoc protocol stack', IEEE Personal Communications, vol. 4, no. 5, pp. 8-15.

39. Gossain, H, Nandiraju, N, Anand, K andAgrawal, DP 2004, 'Supporting MAC layer multicast in IEEE 802.11 based MANETs: issues and solutions', In Proceedings of the Conference on Local Computer Networks (LCN '04), pp. 172-179.

40. Gui, C andMohapatra, P 2003, 'Efficient overlay multicast for mobile ad hoc networks', In Proceedings of the IEEE Wireless Communications and Networking Conference (WCNC '03), vol. 2, pp. 1118-1123.

41. Guoyou He, 2002, 'Destination-sequenced distance vector (DSDV) protocol', Technical report, Helsinki University of Technology, Finland.

42. Hang Zhang, Xi Wang, ParisaMemarmoshrefi, Dieter Hogrefe, 2017, ' A survey of Ant Colony Optimization Based Routing Protocols for Mobile Ad Hoc Networks', IEEE Access, Volume 5, pp. 24139-24161.

43. Heinzelman, WB, Chandrakasan, AP andBalakrishnan, H 2002, 'An application-specific protocol architecture for wireless microsensor networks', IEEE Trans. on Wireless Communication, vol. 1, no. 4, pp. 660-670.

44. Houand Li, VOK 1986, 'Transmission Range Control in Multihop Packet Radio Networks', IEEE Transactions on Communications, vol. 34, no. 1, pp. 38-44.

45. Hu, CC, Wu, EHK and Chen, GH 2006, 'OGHAM: on demand global hosts for mobile ad-hocmulticast services', Ad Hoc Networks, vol. 4, no. 6, pp. 709-723.

46. IETF MANETWorking Group, http://www.ietf.org.

47. Jain, S and Das, SR 2006, 'MAC layer multicast in wireless multihop networks', In Proceedings of the 1st International Conference on Communication System Software and Middleware (Comsware '06), pp. 1-10.

48. Jetcheva, JG and Johnson, DB 2001, 'Adaptive demand-driven multicast routing in multi-hop wireless ad hoc networks', In Proceedings of the 2nd ACM International Symposium on Mobile Ad Hoc Networking and Computing (MobiHoc '01), pp. 33-44.

49. Ji, L and Corson, MS 2001, 'Differential destination multicasta MANET multicast routing protocol for small groups', In Proceedings of the 20th Annual Joint Conference of the IEEE Computer and Communications Societies (INFOCOM'01), vol. 2, pp. 1192-1201.

50. Jiang, S, He, D. andRao, J, 2001, 'A Prediction-based Link Availability Estimation for Mobile Ad Hoc Networks', In Proceedings of IEEE INFOCOM, vol.3, pp. 1745-1752.

51. Jochen Schiller 2000, Mobile Communications. Addison-Wesley.

52. Johnson, D andMaltz, D 1996, 'Dynamic source routing in ad hoc wireless networks', In Mobile Computing, Imielinski T, Korth H (eds). Kluwer Academic, pp. 153-181.

53. Jubin, J andTornow, J 1987, 'The DARPA packet radio network protocols', In Proceedings of the IEEE, vol. 75, no. 1, pp. 21-32.

54. Junhai, L, Liu, X andDanxia, Y 2008, 'Research on multicast routing protocols for mobile ad-hoc networks', Computer Networks, vol. 52, no. 5, pp. 988-997.

55. Kamerman, A andMonteban, L 1997, 'Wave LAN-II: a high-performance wireless LAN for the unlicensed band', Bell Labs Technical Journal, pp. 118-133.

56. Khan, J, Hyder, SI andFakar, SM 2011, 'Modeling and simulation of dynamic intermediate nodes and performance analysis in MANETs reactive routing protocol,' International Journal of Grid and Distributed Computing, vol. 4, no. 1, pp. 31-56.

57. Kim, KI and Kim, SH 2005, 'DESIRE: density aware heterogenous overlay multicast forwarding scheme in mobile ad hoc networks', IEICE Transactions on Communications, vol. E88- B, no. 9, pp. 3579-3586.

58. Kim, S and Lee, K 2008, 'A study on the advanced inference routing network scheme for RODMRP', In Proceedings of the IEEE International conference on Advanced Language Processing and Web Information Technology, pp. 313-314.

59. Kuppusamy, P, Thirunavukkarsu, K andKalavathi, B 2011, 'A study and Comparison of OLSR, AODV and TORA Routing Protocols in Ad hoc Networks', In 3rd IEEE Conference on Electronics Computer Technology (ICECT 2011), pp. 8- 10.

60. Lal, C, Laxmi, V and Gaur, MS 2011, 'Performance Analysis of MANET Routing Protocols for Multimedia Traffic', In 2nd IEEE International Conference on Computer and Communication Technology (ICCCT), pp. 595-600.

61. Laura Marie Feeney 1999, 'A taxonomy for routing protocols in mobile ad hoc networks', Technical report, Swedish Institute of Computer Science, Sweden.

62. LaxmiShrivastava, Sarita S Bhadauria andTomar, GS 2011, 'Performance Evaluation of Routing Protocols in MANET with different traffic loads', In IEEE Conference on Communication Systems and Network Technologies, pp. 13-16.

63. Lee, M and Kim, Y K 2001, 'PatchODMRP: an ad hoc multicast routing protocol', In Proceedings of the International Conference on Information Networking, pp. 537-543.

64. Lee, S and Kim, C 2000, 'Neighbor supporting ad hoc multicast routing protocol', In Proceedings of the ACM International Symposium on Mobile Ad Hoc Networking and Computing (MobiHoc '00), pp. 37-44.

65. Lee, SJ, Su, W andGerla, M 2002, 'On-demand multicast routing protocol in multihop wireless mobile networks', Mobile Networks and Applications, vol. 7, no. 6, pp. 441-453.

66. Li, Q, Aslam, J andRus, D 2001, 'Online power-aware routing in wireless ad-hoc networks', In Proceedings of International Conference on Mobile Computing and Networking (MobiCom'2001), pp. 97-107.

67. M.Haenggi, 2004, ' Routing in Ad Hoc Networks – A Wireless Perspective', In Proceedings of First International Conference on Broadband Networks, pp. 652-660.

68. Manveen Singh Chadha, RanbirJoon andSandeep, 2012, 'Simulation and Comparison of AODV, DSR and AOMDV Routing Protocols in MANETs', International Journal of Soft Computing and Engineering, vol. 2, no. 3, pp. 375-381.

69. Mohammad M. Qabajeh, Aisha H.Abdalla, Othman O.Khalifa, Liana K.Qabajeh, 2015, ' A Survey on Scalable Multicasting in Mobile Ad Hoc Networks', An International Journal of Wireless Personal Communications, vol. 80 issue 1, pp. 369-393.

70. Mohammed Saghir, Tat-CheeWan andRahmatBudiarto 2006, 'QoS Multicast Routing Based on Bandwidth Estimation in Mobile Ad Hoc Networks', In Proceedings of the Int. Conf. on Computer and Communication Engineering (ICCCE), vol. 1, pp. 9-11.

71. Moustafa, H andLabiod, H 2002, 'SRMP: a mesh-based protocol for multicast communication in ad hoc networks', In Proceedings of the International Conference on Third Generation Wireless and Beyond 3Gwireless, pp. 43-48.

72. Muhammad Shaffatul Islam, Md Adnan Riaz and Mohammed Tarique 2012, 'Performance analysis of the routing protocols for video streaming over Mobile ad hoc networks', International Journal of Computer Networks and Communications, vol. 4, no. 3, pp. 133-150.

73. Muhammad Shaffatul Islam, Md.AdnanRiaz, Mohammed Tarique, 2012,' Performance Analysis of Routing Protocols of Mobile Ad Hoc Networks for VoIP Appliccations', Cyber Journals: Multidisciplinary Journals in Science and Technology, Journal of Selected Areas in Telecommunications (JSAT), June Edition, pp. 26-33.

74. Murthy, CSR andManoj, BS 2004, 'Ad Hoc Wireless Networks: Architectures and Protocols', Prentice-Hall, Upper Saddle River, NJ, USA.

75. Narayanan, S and Rani Thotungal 2013, 'Cross Layer Based Routing and Rate Control using Fuzzy Decision System in MANET', International Review on Computer and Software, vol. 18, no. 2, pp. 642-652.

76. Nguyen, UT andXiong, X 2005, 'Rate-adaptive multicast in mobile ad-hoc networks', In IEEE International Conference on Wireless and Mobile Computing, Networking and Communications (WiMob '05), vol. 3, pp. 352-360.

77. Nicola Baldo and Michele Zorzi 2008, 'Fuzzy Logic for Cross-layer Optimization in Cognitive Radio Networks', IEEE Communications Magazine, vol. 46, no. 4, pp. 64-71.

78. Nicola Baldoand Michele Zorzi. 2008, 'Fuzzy Logic for Cross-layer Optimization in Cognitive Radio Networks', IEEE Communications Magazine, vol. 46, no. 4, pp. 64-71.

79. Ozaki, T, Kim, JB andSuda, T 2001, 'Bandwidth-efficient multicast routing for multihop, ad-hoc wireless networks', In Proceedings of the 20th Annual Joint Conference of the IEEE Computer and Communications Societies (INFOCOM'01), vol. 2, pp. 1182-1191.

80. Papavassiliou, S and An, B 2002, 'Supporting multicasting in mobile ad-hoc wireless Networks: Issues, Challenges, and Current Protocols', Wireless Communications and Mobile Computing, vol. 2, no. 2, pp. 115-130.

81. Park, S and Park, D 2004, 'Adaptive core multicast routing protocol," Wireless Networks', vol. 10, no. 1, pp. 53-60.

82. Parul Sharma, ArvindKalia andJawahar Thakur, 2012, 'Performance analysis of AODV, DSR and DSDV Routing Protocols in Mobile Adhoc Networks (MANET)', Journal of Information Systems and Communication, vol. 3, no. 1, pp. 322 - 326.

83. Pei, G, Gerla, M and Chen, TW 2000, 'Fish eye state routing: a routing scheme for ad hoc wireless networks', In Proceedings of IEEE International Conference on Communications (ICC) 2000, pp. 70-74.

84. Perkins, C andBhagwat, P 1994, 'Highly dynamic destination sequenced distance-vector routing (DSDV) for mobile computers', Computer Communications Review, vol. 24, no. 4, pp. 234-244.

85. Perkins, C and Royer, E 1999, 'Ad-hoc on-demand distance vector routing', In 2nd IEEE Workshop on Mobile Computing Systems and Applications, pp. 90-100.

86. Perkins, C 2000, 'Ad-Hoc Networking', Addison-Wesley, Reading, Mass, USA.

87. Perkins, CE 1997, 'Ad Hoc On Demand Distance Vector (AODV) Routing', Internet-Draft, draft-ietf-manet-aodv-00.txt.

88. Pompili, D andVittucci, M 2006, 'PPMA, a probabilistic predictive multicast algorithm for ad hoc networks', Ad Hoc Networks, vol. 4, no. 6, pp. 724-748.

89. PrabhugoudBasarkod and Sunil Manvi, 2014. ' On Demand Bandwidth and Stability Based Unicast Routing in Mobile Ad Hoc Networks', International Journal of Electronics and Telecommunications, vol.60(1), pp. 27-39.

90. Pragati, E andRajenderNath 2012, 'Performance evaluation of AODV, LEACH, TORA protocols through simulation', International journal of advanced research in computer science and software engineering, vol. 2, no. 7, pp. 84-89.

91. Prasad, G N V, Siva Parvathi, V andNageswaraRao, K 2011, 'Link stability based multicast routing scheme in MANET', International Journal of Advanced Engineering Sciences and Technologies (IJAEST), vol. 8, no. 2, pp. 169-176.

92. PrasunSinha, R. S and Bharghavan V, 1999, 'MCEDAR: multicast core-extraction distributed Ad Hoc routing', In Proceedings of the Wireless Communications and Networking Conference, vol. 3, pp. 1313–1317.

93. PrasunSinha, RS andBharghavan, V 1999, 'MCEDAR: multicast core-extraction distributed ad hoc routing', In Proceedings of the Wireless Communications and Networking Conference, vol. 3, pp. 1313-1317.

94. Qian Zhang andYa-Qin Zhang 2008, 'Cross-Layer Design for QoS Support in Multihop Wireless Networks', In Proceedings of the IEEE, vol. 96, no. 1.

95. Rahman, J,Hasan, M, Mehedi, A, Islam, M and Ben, K 2012, 'Comparative analysis the performance of AODV, DSDV and DSR routing protocols in wireless sensor network', In 7th International Conference on Electrical and Computer Engineering (ICECE), pp. 283-286.

96. Ramanathan, R and Rosales-Hain, R 2000, 'Topology control of multihop wireless networks using transmit power adjustment', In Proceedings of the Conference on Computer Communications (IEEE Infocom 2000) pp. 404-413.

97. Rolf Winter, Jochen H Schiller, NavidNikaeinand Christian Bonnet. 2006, 'CrossTalk: Cross-Layer Decision Support Based on Global Knowledge', IEEE Communications Magazine, vol. 44, no. 1, pp. 93-99.

98. Royer, EM and Perkins, CE 2000, 'Multicast ad hoc on demand distance vector (MAODV) routing', Internet-Draft, draft-ietfdraft-maodv-00.txt, 2000.

99. Rudolph, V andMeng, TH 1999, 'Minimum energy mobile wireless networks', IEEE Journal of Selected Areas in Communications, vol. 17, no. 8, pp. 1333-1344.

100. Saiful Azad M,ArafaturRahman, Farhat Anwar, 2007, 'A Performance Comparison of Proactive and Reactive Routing Protocols of Mobile Ad Hoc Network', Journal of Engineering and Applied Sciences, vol. 2, no. 5, pp. 891-896.

101. Sajama and Haas, ZJ 2003, 'Independent-tree ad hoc multicast routing (ITAMAR)', Mobile Networks and Applications, vol. 8, no. 5, pp. 551-566.

102. SambhuDahai, Niranjan Ray, 2016, Enchanced Multicast Routing Protocol in MANET', In Proceedings of the International Conference on Information Technology (ICIT'2016), pp. 6-11.

103. Sanchez, M, Manzoni, P and Haas, ZH 1999, 'Determination of critical transmission range in ad-hoc networks', In Proceedings of Multiaccess, Mobility and Teletraffic for Wireless Communications (MMT'99).

104. Santi, P 2005, 'Topology control in wireless ad hoc and sensor networks', London: John Wiley & Sons, Ltd.

105. Shanthi, G andAlameluNachiappan 2012, 'Fuzzy - cost based multiconstrainedQoS routing with mobility prediction in MANETs', Egyptian Informatics Journal, vol. 13, pp. 19-25.

106. Shen, CC andJaikaeo, C 2005, 'Ad hoc multicast routing algorithm with swarm intelligence', Mobile Networks and Applications, vol. 10, no. 1, pp. 47-59.

107. Si, W and Li, C 2004, 'RMAC: a reliable multicast MAC protocol for wireless ad hoc networks', In Proceedings of the International Conference on Parallel Processing (ICPP '04), pp. 494-501.

108. Sisodia, RS, Karthigeyan, I, Manoj, BS and Murthy, CSR 2003, 'A preferred link based multicast protocol for wireless mobile ad hoc networks', In Proceedings of the IEEE International Conference on Communications (ICC '03), vol. 3, pp. 2213-2217.

109. Stanze, O andZitterbart, M 2005, 'On-demand overlay multicast in mobile ad hoc networks', In Proceedings of the IEEE Wireless Communications and Networking Conference (WCNC '05), vol. 4, pp. 2155-2161.

110. Stojmenovic, I and Lin, X 2001, 'Power-aware localized routing in wireless networks', IEEE Transactions on Parallel and Distributed Systems vol. 12, no. 11, pp. 1122-1133.

111. Sujatha V Mallapur andSiddarama R Patil 2015, ''Fuzzy Logic Based Trusted Candidate Selection for Stable Multipath Routing', International Journal of Information Technology and Computer Science, vol. 06, pp. 12-21.

112. Sun, MT, Huang, L, Wang, S, Arora, A and Lai, TH 2003, 'Reliable MAC layer multicast in IEEE 802.11 wireless networks', Wireless Communications and Mobile Computing, vol. 3, no. 4, pp. 439-453.

113. Tang K and M. Gerla,2000, 'Random Access MAC for Efficient Broadcast Support in Ad Hoc Networks', In Proceedings of IEEE Wireless Communication and Networking Conference 2000, pp. 454-459.

114. Tang, K andGerla, M 2000, 'Random access MAC for efficient broadcast support in ad hoc networks', In Proceedings of the IEEE Wireless Communications and Networking Conference (WCNC '00), vol. 1, pp. 454-459.

115. Tang, K andGerla, M 2001, 'MAC reliable broadcast in ad hoc networks', In Proceedings of the IEEE Military Communications Conference (MILCOM '01), vol. 2, pp. 1008-1013.

116. Tang, K andGerla, M 2003, 'Congestion control multicast in wireless ad hoc networks', Computer Communications, vol. 26, no. 3, pp. 278-288.

117. Tobagi, FA andKleinrock, L 1975, 'Packet switching in radio channels - Part II: the hidden terminal problem in carrier sense multiple-access and the busy-tone solution', IEEE Transactions on Communications,

vol. 23, no. 12, pp. 1417- 1433.

118. Toh, CK 2002, 'Ad Hoc Mobile Wireless Networks: Protocols and Systems', Prentice-Hall, Englewood Cliffs, NJ, USA.

119. Toh, CK, Guichal, G andBunchua, S 2000, 'ABAM: on-demand associativity-based multicast routing for ad hoc mobile networks', In Proceedings of the IEEE Vehicular Technology Conference (VTC '00), vol. 3, pp. 987-993.

120. Vaishampayan, R and Garcia-Luna-Aceves, JJ 2004, 'Protocol for unified multicasting through announcements (PUMA)', In IEEE International Conference on Mobile Ad- Hoc and Sensor Systems (MASS '04), pp. 1906-1912.

121. Wang, X, Li, F, Ishihara, S and Mizuno, T 2001, 'A multicast routing algorithm based on mobile multicast agents in ad-hoc networks', IEICE Transactions on Communications, vol. E84-B, no. 8, pp. 2087-2094.

122. Wang, Z, Liang, Y and Wang, L 2008, 'Multicast in mobile ad hoc networks', In IFIP International Federation for Information Processing, vol. 258, pp. 151-164.

123. Wattenhofer, R, Li, L, Bahl, P and Wang, YM 2001, 'Distributed topology control for power efficient operation in multihop wireless ad hoc networks', In Proceedings of the Conference on Computer Communications (IEEE Infocom 2001), pp. 1388-1397.

124. Woesner, H, Ebert, JP, Schlager, M andWolisz, A 1998, 'Power-saving mechanisms in emerging standards for wireless LANs: the MAC level perspective', IEEE Personal Communications, vol. 5, no. 3, pp. 40-48.

125. Wu, CW, Tay, YC andToh, CK 2000, 'Ad hocMulticast Routing protocol utilizing Increasing id-numbers (AMRIS)', draftietf-manet-amris-spec-00.txt.

126. Xie, J, Talpade, RR, McAuley, A and Liu, M 2002, 'AMRoute: ad hoc multicast routing protocol', Mobile Networks and Applications, vol. 7, no. 6, pp. 429-439.

127. Xu, Y, Heidemann, J andEstrin, D 2001, 'Geography-informed energy conservation for ad hoc routing', Proceedings of International

Conference on Mobile Computing and Networking (Mobi-Com'2001), pp. 70-84.

128. Young-junand Kang-Whan Lee 2017, 'Energy-efficient and reliable routing protocol for dynamic-property-based clustering mobile ad hoc networks', International Journal of Distributed Sensor Networks, vol. 13, no. 1, pp. 1-16.

129. Young-jun oh, Kang – whan Lee, 2017, 'Energy-Efficient And Reliable Routing Protocol For Dynamic-Property-Based Clustering Mobile Ad Hoc Networks', International Journal of Distributed Sensor Networks, vol.13, no. 1, pp. 1-16.

130. Younis, O andFahmy, S 2004, 'HEED: a hybrid, energy-efficient, distributed clustering approach for ad-hoc sensor networks', IEEE Transactions on Mobile Computing, vol. 3, no. 4, pp. 366-379.

131. Yufang Zhu and Thomas Kunz 2004, 'MAODV Implementation for NS-2.26', Systems and Computing Engineering, Carleton University, Technical Report SCE-04-01.

132. ZeeshanIqbal, Khan, S, AmjadMehmood, Jaime Lloret and Nabil Ali Alrajeh 2016, 'Adaptive Cross-Layer Multipath Routing Protocol for Mobile Ad Hoc Networks', Journal of Sensors, vol. 2016, Article ID. 5486437, pp. 1-18.

133. Zhang, X and Jacob, L 2004, 'MZRP: an extension of the zone routing protocol for multicasting in MANETs', Journal of Information Science and Engineering, vol. 20, no. 3, pp. 535-551.

134. Zhu, J, Qiao, C and Wang, X 2004, ' A Comprehensive Minimum Energy Routing Scheme for Wireless Ad Hoc Networks', In proceedings of IEEE INFOCOM 2004, vol 3,pp. 2800-2811.

www.ingramcontent.com/pod-product-compliance
Lightning Source LLC
LaVergne TN
LVHW082334200926
848481LV00012B/3345
9798232062293